"Our day and age truly needs writers who can share their spiritual journey in a way that is both convincing and moving. Edward Sellner does just that. In the midst of scholarly research he lets us know how it challenges and changes him. Such frankness and spiritual sensitivity are seldom shared in our day."

Most Reverend Rembert G. Weakland, O.S.B.
Archbishop of Milwaukee

"*Soul-Making* is at once a journey backwards through time to the long-lost world of Celtic spirituality and 'soul-friendship,' and the author's journey made in the present through the challenging, tangled, and wonderful world of family relationships. Sellner's journey is made in exile—and in the day-by-day loneliness of exile—and this is used skillfully and impressively as a pathway toward understanding the spiritual harvest that comes to the Celtic saints through solitude and exile. It is a fresh and lively way of bringing research to life; Patrick, Columba, Brigit, and, above all, Cuthbert become real companions not only as imaginatively recalled but as mystically present, startlingly so at times.

"Professor Sellner's moving book opens a doorway into that Celtic past and discovers a far-off source of clear and steady light that can, as this book bears witness, serve to illumine the present at a time when so many lights, old and new, seem to be fading."

Noel Dermot O'Donoghue, O.D.C.
Author of *Mystics for Our Time*

"Edward Sellner has woven together his long pilgrimage to the British Isles with history, theology, psychology, and personal memory. His honest personal commentary and unusual adventures stimulate the reader's own sense of personal confrontation, grace, and discovery that are classic marks of spiritual pilgrimage."

Tilden Edwards, Executive Director,
Shalem Institute for Spiritual Formation

"Edward Sellner's *Soul-Making* is an intensely personal account of his outward journey through England, Ireland, and Wales and his inward journey into greater spiritual wholeness on the other side of the midlife crisis. This book will be of interest to many persons. It provides a graphic description of the wonders of Oxford, Ireland, and Wales, especially of those places connected with the 'holy ones' of those lands. It offers insights into the history and wisdom of Celtic spirituality, serving as a valuable resource for those drawn to this tradition. Finally, it holds appeal to those in midlife who struggle to come to terms with loneliness, ego-needs, personal integration, and prayer.

"*Soul-Making* is written in a direct and engaging style. The reader is invited to tread the ways of land and sea, psyche and spirit; to encounter the lively presence of ancestors and saints such as Patrick, Brigit, and Columcille; to attend to dreams and to one's most treasured relationships; to wrestle with the vision of John Henry Newman and the needs of the contemporary church. Soul-friends are recognized in the ordinary and unexpected encounters of one's life. They serve as mid-wives and pointers to ever deeper levels of personal and communal wholeness. Sellner's journal invites readers to attend to their own inward and outward journey of soul-making."

Elizabeth Dreyer, Washington Theological Union
Author of *Passionate Women* and
Manifestations of Grace

"This journey of an American soul and theologian through Europe captures much of the Spiritual Journey of all Christians and provides an inspiring personal example of theologizing on the way."

Enda McDonagh
Moral Theologian
Maynooth, Ireland

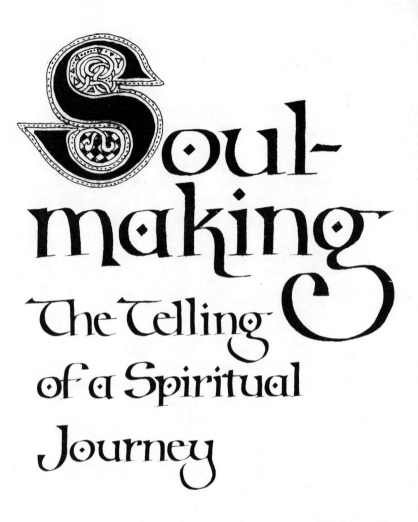

Soul-making

The Telling of a Spiritual Journey

Edward Sellner

TWENTY-THIRD PUBLICATIONS

Mystic, Connecticut 06355

Twenty-Third Publications
185 Willow Street
P.O. Box 180
Mystic, CT 06355
(203) 536-2611
800-321-0411

ISBN 0-89622-457-0
Library of Congress Catalog Card Number 90-71376

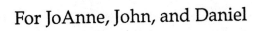
For JoAnne, John, and Daniel

CONTENTS

In epic literature the journey is symbolic of the life of the soul, the cycle of experience which it must undergo.... The telling of our journeys is as much a religion as the ceremonies themselves.

John Sharkey, *Celtic Mysteries*

An ait a bhfuil do chroi is ann a thabharfas do chosa thu.
Your feet will bring you to where your heart is.

Ancient Irish Proverb

INTRODUCTION

In August 1988, while on a leave of absence from teaching, I moved without my family to Oxford, England, to do research for a book on the historical origins of the Celtic soul-friend tradition of spiritual guidance. I intended to do my work at the Bodleian Library, meet regularly with Sr. Benedicta Ward, a scholar in early and medieval church history, and live at the St. Theosevia Centre of Christian Spirituality, an ecumenical center established to promote the study of spiritual traditions, especially Eastern Orthodox and Celtic. While continuing my research, I planned to teach a graduate course at St. Patrick's College, Maynooth, Ireland, during the month of October. Although I never consciously stated it as an objective, in the back of my mind I also hoped to visit various holy places associated with the Celtic saints in order to write more clearly about the wisdom figures and geographical and spiritual landscape of the Early Celtic Church.

The longer I stayed thousands of miles from my family, friends, and colleagues in the States, the more I began to empathize with those early Irish missionaries and wandering scholars who for the sake of the gospel faced the loneliness of being far from their homeland and friends—for, of course, much longer periods of time than mine. As I did my research, moving from place to place that fall and meeting with scholars and ordinary people along the way, the more I also began to feel like one of those ancient visitors to Egypt who were profoundly affected by the wisdom of the early Desert Christians they encountered there. My journeys to Celtic lands, I came to realize, were having a significant effect on me, leading me to new awarenesses about spirituality, in general, as it is being lived in Ireland and Great Britain, especially among the laity, and, in particular, a new awareness about myself. Like those early pilgrims Jerome, Melania, Rufinus, Palladius, Cassian, and Germanus, who had learned much from going into the desert regions centuries ago, I gradually became aware of how much I wanted to bring back and share with others what I was learning. One evening in Ireland, while rereading the journal I had begun when I arrived at Oxford, I came to the conclusion that other people might gain from it insight into their own self-understanding and spirituality.

This book, then, is not the historical one I anticipated writing, but it is about what I unexpectedly encountered on my journeys that fall. It takes the form of a personal journal, and contains my reflections upon those vivid experiences that taught me much more than I could have imagined as I began my sojourn abroad. Cut off from the normal social supports of family, job, colleagues, and friends, I entered a kind of solitude I had not expected, and I was faced even more persistently with questions that had arisen earlier when I was entering midlife. As my journal entries reveal, my journeys to Celtic lands became in many unforeseen ways an encounter with my deeper self and with a loving God whose existence I had come to doubt. My travels became a form of pilgrimage as I discovered firsthand that the holy places and the tombs of the saints provide a location for the healing, forgiving, and guiding powers of God.

The Irish have an ancient tradition they call "soul-making," reviewing the direction of one's life and eventually attempting to make peace with the physical and the spiritual worlds, so closely connected, and our place within them. This reconciliation process necessarily involves self-confrontation and the courage to change, and, as such, can be especially disturbing and anxiety-provoking. It can induce and often does bring out a great deal of grief, anger, and rage. Yet, in the long run, soul-making is most rewarding, for it can teach us wisdom, compassion, and, when we have gotten some distance from the pain, gratitude for all that has been a part of that reconciliation process—even the depths of our despair.

Soul-making is the crucial task when we reach midlife. Although similar to all of life's major transitions, that rite of passage especially is a time of struggle, of deep and aching pain, of the unmasking of illusions. It is definitely a journey into the unknown. It is as if we awake one day and find ourselves in a strange land, a foreign territory, a twilight zone where traditional roles, old perceptions, and comfortable habits no longer seem to fit. Like Alice in Wonderland or the children of Narnia, what we find through the looking glass or behind the wardrobe door can fill us initially with wonder and amazement. These early responses, however, soon give way to confusion over the strange beasts encountered in those mysterious lands, as well as the terror of our own powerlessness.

We discover the need to acknowledge, accept, and integrate inner polarities we didn't know existed. We find that forgotten wounds from early childhood *and* fears of growing old can no longer be repressed. We become excited about new ideas and dreams yet to be fulfilled, *and* we feel guilty for destructive behaviors inflicted often upon those we love the most as we search for new expressions of our creativity. We want to belong *and* we yearn for solitude. We are pulled between qualities and states-of-being that in the past were associated exclusively with the "masculine" or the "feminine," but by midlife can no longer be so easily dichotomized. We come to see that we must be both assertive *and* gentle, just *and* compassionate, nurturing *and* challenging of those people and institutions we love. Most of all, in our search for wisdom we find, as did the French writer Pascal, that truth is discerned "not only through our reason but also through our heart."[1]

---

[1] Pascal, *Pensees* (New York: Penguin Books, 1984), p. 58.

Whatever the length or duration of the journey into midlife, it necessarily involves the painful process of conversion in which one becomes less concerned with recognition, success, and power, and more with the values of self-knowledge, self-acceptance, integrity, generativity. It is a process that can lead to forgiveness and reconciliation, often with one's parents, siblings, spouse, children, friends and enemies alike—but only, it seems, if one begins with oneself. For those who survive, this journey, accompanied as it is by much agony, can also result in the joy associated with giving birth. It can become a pilgrimage toward greater freedom and wholeness when we are given the courage to face the terror of the unknown and to persist, despite all those parts of ourselves, all those relationships and institutions that seem to want us to stay the way we were. Perhaps, most importantly, the journey into midlife, like so many of our crises and transitions, can become a form of pilgrimage when we invite God to join us as our companion, even though that God may seem at the time more antagonist than friend. (In retrospect, we may discover, as Jacob did in his struggle with the angel, that these two forms of relating are not necessarily exclusive roles.)

This process of soul-making, since it must begin with ourselves, is intimately related to the development of our own spirituality, based not so much upon exterior dogmas and formal doctrines as it is on a personal commitment to the search for wisdom and the holy life. Ultimately, it may result in the important ministry of mentoring, for developmental psychologists as well as our Judeo-Christian spiritual traditions believe that, although we can serve various mentoring roles and functions earlier in life, we become mentors in the fuller sense only after reaching our forties or fifties. While we may become better mentors, friends, and spiritual guides at midlife, it is also the experience of many that as we move into midlife help is often found in unexpected people and places along the way.

These benevolent helpers have been identified in various ways by different peoples. The Greeks and Romans believed that every person had a genius, daemon, guardian spirit, or "heavenly twin" which, linked with one's personality and soul through friendship, provided personal care, protection, and guidance. Certain Native American shamans and those of pre-literate peoples identified their spiritual power and vocation of service to the tribe with at least one guardian or tutelary spirit, often acquired in a vision quest in the wilderness. This helpful spirit, frequently identified with some animal, became an alter ego or another self, and was called simply a friend or companion. The Desert Christians of the third, fourth, and fifth centuries in Egypt, Syria, and Palestine looked to each other, as well as to angelic powers, for spiritual guidance and healing—always, of course, placing their ultimate trust in the Holy Spirit. Eastern Orthodox Christians have the tradition of the *staretz*, the wise person, ordained or lay, who acts as a confessor and spiritual director, and whose guidance, frequently in the form of dreams, can continue after his or her death. The Swiss psychiatrist Carl Jung experienced in his personal and professional life the help of what he called "living" and "ghostly gurus," including at least one significant inner guide, Philemon, who appeared in his dreams.[2]

The ancient Celtic Christians had their own tradition of guidance, and a word associated with it: *anamchara*, Gaelic for "friend of the soul," and they believed, as the Early Christian saint and shaman Brigit said, that "anyone without a soul friend is like a body without a head."[3]

Whatever term we prefer to use, these various spiritual traditions clearly reveal resources that can help us on our journeys, certain relationships of intimacy and depth that transcend time and space and death itself: spiritual mentors whom we perhaps have never met in this lifetime, but who definitely can make a difference in the direction of our lives. Such spiritual mentors, as my

---

[2] Carl Jung, *Memories, Dreams, Reflections* (New York: Vintage Books, 1961), p. 181 ff.

[3] See Whitley Stokes, ed., *The Martyrology of Oengus the Culdee* (Dublin: Dublin Institute for Advanced Studies, 1984), p. 65.

journal shows, might include certain dream figures who come to us at night or in the early waking hours, "when our minds, more pilgrim from the flesh," as Dante tells us, "are less imprisoned by the bonds of thought and in their visions have prophetic power."[4] Whenever they appear and in whatever guise they may take or disguise they may wear, the soul makes its presence known at such critical junctures.

Like our life transitions, our travels to foreign lands can be journeys into the unknown, far away from our families and friends and all those people and things that give us a sense of identity and personal worth. Anyone who has traveled abroad can speak of the wonders discovered there, as well as the hardships and at times near-catastrophes associated with those travels. Such journeys, however difficult, can offer insights into our own lives and times. They can give us an understanding when we are far from home of our true priorities and values; perhaps in the most fundamental sense they can teach us who we are. That was my experience living far from those I loved and who loved me. The "soul space" I was given at Oxford, the love and acceptance I received unexpectedly from so many strangers, the holy places I visited in England, Wales, Ireland, and later, Italy—all contributed to my own process of soul-making, teaching me much about my life, myself, and the ongoing reality of love which we Christians associate with the word "God." It also taught me a great deal experientially about soul friendship: not only the friends who act in our lives as spiritual mentors and guides, but about that communion of saints all around us and living within our depths that give us guidance and direction when we call upon them.

Though the details and the journeys described here may differ dramatically from yours, perhaps your experience of pilgrimage and soul-making is similar to mine.

This book could not have been written without the significant contribution of those many friends and acquaintances who are de-

---

[4] Dante Alighieri, *The Divine Comedy* (London: The Folio Society, 1979), p. 185.

scribed or alluded to in my journal. Without their hospitality and
help, my learning experience might have been limited to only
books and library staffs. I am especially grateful to friends in the
States, especially Ken Schmitz, Mary Talcott, Kay VanderVort,
Mary Erickson, Gretchen Berg, and Mark Scannell, who have encouraged me over the years to pursue my research and journeys
to Celtic lands. Mark, my spiritual guide for some years, first suggested that I begin to keep a journal in preparation for eventually
writing a book on the Celtic soul friend. Without his encouragement and continued support, I probably would still be waiting for
the "right moment" before initiating my writing.

I also want to thank four significant mentors in England and
Ireland: Canon A.M. (Donald) Allchin, Anglican writer and ecu-
menist whose warm friendship meant a great deal to me before I
moved to Oxford and while I lived with the community he had
brought together at St. Theosevia's; the historian Sr. Benedicta
Ward, S.L.G., at the Centre for Medieval and Renaissance Studies
in Oxford, who acted in many ways as both a tutor and colleague,
meeting with me weekly to discuss my research; Sr. Helen Columba, S.L.G., whose insights into Celtic spirituality were so intimately linked with her own life and dream experiences on the
holy island of Iona; and Rev. Ronan Drury, editor of the Irish pastoral journal, *The Furrow*, whose special arrangements for me
while I was at St. Patrick's College, Maynooth, made it possible
for me to pursue my research, as well as experience the religious
and cultural life of Ireland. Each of them, in addition to those
many others who will be encountered in the following pages,
made my leave of absence most memorable.

Most of all, I want to thank my wife, JoAnne, and my sons,
John Nicholas and Daniel Patrick, for their allowing me to be
gone while I pursued the daemons of my heart. This book is dedicated to them: JoAnne, who, in the words of Yeats, shares with
me a pilgrim soul, and my sons whom I take with me in my heart
on my pilgrimages to foreign shores. I discovered while I was
away from them, as John Howard Griffin relates in his *Hermitage*

Journals, based on journaling he did while living in Thomas Merton's hermitage, that there definitely is a "kind of tearing" in being away from one's family when a person intensely experiences both "the unblemished joy of solitude" and at the same time a "constant longing" to be with one's wife and children.[5] Absence definitely makes the heart grow fonder, and yet, in the midst of great anguish of soul and body when we are separated from those we love, we also experience at times, most paradoxically, a great communion with them that transcends the miles.

There is another paradox that these pages will reveal: how sometimes our souls can seem most rooted in foreign soil, because they contain, as Jung alludes to in his writings, "ancestral components,"[6] individual elements of soul inherited from our ancestors. Because of this psychic inheritance, many people when first visiting certain foreign shores have an intuitive sense of having been there before, sometimes even an experience of homecoming. That, at least, has been my experience in my visits to the Celtic lands of Ireland, England, Scotland, and Wales. Ireland is, after all, the home of my ancestors who fled County Mayo and the potato famines of the 1840s in order to survive. It is there I sometimes feel most at home: walking in the Wicklow mountains near Glendalough or on the shores of the River Shannon near Clonmacnoise, exploring the sites of Cashel and Downpatrick where St. Patrick once preached, warming myself over a peat-fire at Maynooth after a cold, rainy day, or praying in the Cathedral of Armagh, that beautiful church which in its many artistic expressions reveals so well the rich spiritual heritage of the Christian Celts. In many conscious and unconscious ways, Ireland for me, as one of her poets once said, is the center of my longings, the home of my heart. On my visits to Ireland, as well as to certain Celtic holy places like Iona in Scotland, Lindisfarne in England, and St. David's in Wales,

---

[5] John Howard Griffin, *The Hermitage Journals* (Kansas City: Andrews and McMeel, Inc.), pp. 89–90.

[6] See Jung, *Memories, Dreams, Reflections*, pp. 235–236.

I have often experienced glimpses of the eternal, a joy that the English writer C.S. Lewis calls "a pointer to something else."[7]

I hope my sons, in particular, and you, the reader, will also find that experience of joy and of the sacred in your lives—if not in Celtic lands, then in some other places made holy by people who discern and celebrate God's loving presence in their lives. I hope your feet will take you to where your heart is, and that your pilgrimages of the heart will help you discern the powerful presence of the soul.

---

[7] C.S. Lewis, *Surprised by Joy: The Shape of My Early Life* (New York: Harcourt, Brace & World, Inc., 1955), p. 238.

✳ 1 ✳

A PLACE OF LOOSENING CHAINS
August 25-31, 1988

We are not wholly brute. To us remains
A clean, sweet city lulled by ancient streams,
A place of vision and of loosening chains....

C. S. Lewis, "Oxford"

Thursday, August 25

I am here in Oxford at last, after a year of doubts, uncertainties, and immense frustrations as I wondered if I would ever make it. As it was, things finally seemed to begin to fall into place this spring when JoAnne's crippling illness disappeared and I was given tenure at the college. By summer I was no longer so involved in national lay ministry concerns, freeing up more time for me to teach and write—what I have been wanting to do for so long. Even at the last minute before I left home, I received some financial assistance from Irish-American patrons interested in sponsoring my research.

Synchronicity has been happening since my arrival this morning at Gatwick in the early waking hours. I unexpectedly got help by seeing a sign about a train that goes directly to Oxford instead of going into London first and then getting one out; I received assistance from a porter at the Reading station who put me on the right train with all my luggage and books; I got help when the taxi dropped me off in front of the St. Theosevia Centre only to find an elderly woman, Mrs. Militza Zernov, just leaving the house. She welcomed me warmly and let me in (thank God!), since everyone else was gone for the day. If she had not been there, I would have spent the entire day waiting....I deposited my things in a wonderful room overlooking a garden, in this old Victorian mansion on Canterbury Road, between Woodstock and Banbury, about a twenty-minute walk—I've discovered—from the center of Oxford.

I left immediately for High Street and Broad Street to see the Greco-Roman "faces" surrounding the Sheldonian and, of course, Blackwells, the best-known bookstore in all of England. Again, it was as if someone were guiding me by the hand, for a book on Celtic history that I had been attempting to find this past year fairly jumped down at me from the shelf. Then, back at the center, when I had about given up on seeing any friendly faces, Manus, one of the residents preparing his supper in the kitchen, invited me to share his food. It was an unexpected act of hospitality to a stranger from a stranger which I greatly appreciated, as well as the conversation introducing me to the house and its residents.

You have been with me, Lord, and, though I am feeling exhausted from jet lag, I am grateful for this first day away from those I love. Please let this be a worthwhile time apart from JoAnne and the boys, and please keep them safely in your care.

Friday, August 26

I have begun my day with exercises, shower (getting it to work!), shave, coffee, and prayer—asking Jesus to teach me wisdom while I am here. I want to get to know him better these months away, as I go into my own desert retreat experience, and in the process to get to know myself. It seems a long time since I have had much quiet or space in my life for reflection.

For too long I have felt torn between the two sides of me, the activist side seeking church reform and the more contemplative side searching for time to research and write. Ironically, both sides are represented by my two heroes: Robert Kennedy, the politician in whose presidential campaign I worked as a college student, and C.S. Lewis, teacher, writer, spiritual guide whom I came to admire while in graduate school. From Kennedy, I learned about compassion toward the less fortunate and the need for social justice in both society and church. Because of him and the ideals which he taught me, I became active in promoting lay leadership and the full participation of all the baptized in the life of the church. From Lewis's writings, I was given insights about the grief that comes with great loss, about joy that is experienced in our conversions, and about a love that survives all our separations, including death itself. Because of him, I first learned about and eventually visited Oxford, that "sweet city," as Lewis described it in his poetry, "lulled by ancient streams." When I first came here with JoAnne six years ago, I fell in love with it immediately and determined to return someday for a longer stay.

Now I am here at last, and more aware not only how much heroes and mentors can contribute to our lives and the development of our personalities, but also how much inner conflict they can bring. Mine have been at war with each other for some time, and I keep ending up comparing myself with them and what they had already accomplished at my age. Then I find myself at a very deep level constantly "wanting": feeling inadequate, guilty, angry, depressed. Without them, I wouldn't be who I am today, so I need to find a way to integrate, not exterminate them. It is time I began to embrace my life with more joy and gratitude than with the constant frustration, complaint, bitterness and resentments I have been experiencing. Resentments, after all, as I have learned from my work with recovering alcoholics, are the biggest hindrances to spiritual progress. But how to recover joy? How to discover who I am and come to some sort of inner peace within me? This journal, I hope, and my time away will teach me what it is I am to do.

I have been putting together the chronology of events that brought me here, and I am amazed how quickly the decision to make some major life changes came when I turned forty-one. Those changes mysteriously originated in a dream, in the death of my maternal grandmother, and in the story of a saint.

In January 1986, a figure I had never seen before appeared in my dreams wearing ancient green robes, with an exceptionally high forehead. His hair, parted in the middle and dyed a deep scarlet or purple, reached to his shoulders. When the dream figure made his appearance, I did not recognize him nor did I have a name for him. I knew only that, as I heard myself say in the dream, "this is me; this is an image of my Self": the larger personality maturing within, an expression of my soul. In the dream, however, I am so taken aback by the vivid color of the hair that I repart it immediately so that my brown, "more acceptable" hair conceals the scarlet. I awoke from the dream both excited and fascinated by the dream figure, and perplexed by its meaning. Only later did I discover a similar-looking figure, with long hair and brightly-colored cloak, in the *Book of Durrow*, a marvelous mid-seventh-century illuminated Celtic gospel book. According to an art historian, this book was probably created on Lindisfarne, a holy island off the coast of northern England, and it shows the first incontrovertible blending of Irish and Germanic (or Saxon) influence, the very races that make up my family inheritance. I also discovered sometime later that the color of scarlet, a combination of red and purple, symbolizes "the life principle" and "spirituality."

Within a month of that brief, yet very significant dream sequence, Grandma Mary died, my grandmother of Irish ancestry who helped raise me when I was very young. Although her death had been expected and the grief anticipated in my family long before she died at the age of 91, I could not have consciously predicted my response to that great loss. The depths of my grief, however, the night before her burial alerted me for the first time experientially to something which only my dreams had revealed previously. What I sensed, in the outpouring of my tears as I knelt by her coffin after the wake, was an acute awareness of the soul, that dimension of us which transcends our mortal bodies, and yet lies at the very core of our personalities, imaginations, and sensitivity; that part of us that in many ways exists outside the parameters our minds have created regarding space and time. Kneeling there alone in prayer, I remembered St. Augustine's description of true friendship as the experience of one soul in two bodies, two persons united by great love.

I now perceive how the Celtic dream figure and the death of Grandma Mary with whom I so closely identified my sense of Irish heritage were the beginnings of a midlife transition inviting me to take stock of my life. Both experiences have led me here on a search for roots: personal, theological, spiritual; both also helped clarify the crucial questions of midlife that were becoming increasingly difficult for me to ignore: how was I spending my life, my time, my talents and energies; what did I want to do with them in the time I have left; why am I so unhappy?

About six months after the dream and the death of my grandparent, I read Bede the Venerable's *Life of Cuthbert*, the story of a saint who lived on Lindisfarne during the seventh century. This Anglo-Saxon holy man, immersed in a Celtic spirituality taught to him by his spiritual mentor, had been prior of a religious community on that "Holy Island" for some time when he decided to resign his administrative duties at the age of forty-one in order to go into solitude and eventually become a spiritual guide. I had never read anything about Cuthbert before, but, as I read about his decision to resign, it was as if, for the first time, I realized that I too had some options besides the continuing frustration of trying to balance increased administrative duties at the college with my desire to do more teaching and writing. It was as if, by reading this story about a saint who had followed the call of life to his soul, that I was given permission to do the same.

By July of that year, shortly after reading about Cuthbert, I sent a letter to my theology colleagues requesting a change of status at the college; in August I took a trip to Iona, Melrose, Durham, and Lindisfarne, those holy places associated with early Celtic Christianity and Cuthbert's life and ministry. That fall the college agreed to my eventually moving to full-time teaching, especially in the area of Christian spirituality. By Easter 1987 I had communicated with Benedicta Ward at Oxford about a planned sabbatical that would allow me time to do more research; in August of the same year, while presenting a paper at a patristics conference in Oxford, I visited the St. Theosevia Centre, which she had recommended to me. When Canon Donald Allchin, director of the center and long-time friend of Thomas Merton, invited me to stay at St. Theosevia's, I felt as if this is what I was suppose to do. A year later, despite all sorts of unexpected conflicts that seemed to be overwhelming obstacles, I am here.

I needed to come; I needed to get away for awhile, not only for the professional purposes of research, but also for personal reasons. I have not fully recovered from my involvement in so many administrative and ministerial activities the past few years, and I am deeply depressed, wondering if the institutional church will ever change, becoming more responsive to the pastoral needs of the people and more inclusive in its ministries. Vatican II brought with it so much hope, and now the church seems to be going backward, re-establishing old patterns of behavior and of attitudes, while seeming to resist any attempts at significant change. I find myself asking more often than before if I want to remain part of a church that seems at least a hundred years behind the times; and, if I do, how to bring about change in our lifetime, not centuries from now. I want a church much more inclusive of women and lay people's gifts, one based upon respect for diversity and mutual trust, not a church that seems to be becoming increasingly authoritarian and reactionary, relying more upon intimidation than upon inspiration. Both JoAnne and I are also concerned about our sons and what sort of attitudes they will learn from a church that excludes women from decision making and priest-hood.

More basically, as I expressed to Mark before I left, the past year has raised for me fundamental existential and religious questions clearly intertwined with my understanding of the church. The existential question is: can one person make a significant difference or any difference, really, in an institution that consistently seems to resist any change that might threaten those "in control"? Robert Kennedy said that, yes, each of us can make a difference, can have a positive effect. On my good days, I recall his words and believe them; on the bad days, I remember the words of a commentator, after Bobby's assassination, who said that it was only the assassins of him, his brother John, and Martin Luther King, Jr., who truly verified how much difference one person can make.

The religious question that all of my experiences have raised is even more fundamental: is there really a loving God—or a God at all? Yes, I have continued to pray and continued attempting to make sense out of my experiences this past year, but on the affective level God has seemed very far from me much of the time. I realize that one cannot and should not equate God totally with one's feelings, but I cannot ignore the strong feelings of absence nor those at times of anger and betrayal.

I don't have answers to those questions, and most of the time I've felt too tired and depressed to even try.

That's why I needed to come here now, I think. I have been too busy, and perhaps I have been playing too many roles, too many parts, living them all out as duties. I only hope time away will provide some clarity.

Coming here couldn't have been possible without the cooperation of JoAnne. Who else would have agreed to my being gone and also caring for two small children at home? I did ask her if she would come with me, and she said that it was impossible to get off work for that length of time. And when I suggested that perhaps I could bring the boys with me, she said, "You'll never get anything done if you do." I am grateful for her willingness to let me pursue my research without a great burden of guilt, although she, of course, did say that I would "owe" her a great deal upon my return!

Despite the unpleasant memories of the past year, what I am feeling here thus far is soul space: space for quiet and reflection; space to drink deeply of the solitude, as if at a holy well of regeneration. I finally have a room above a beautiful garden to look out upon, with the bells from the Greek and Russian Orthodox church next door ringing on the hour (their sounds appreciated for the most part, except when they begin at 6 in the morning!).

Saturday, August 27

The white martyrdom of Irish *peregrini*, according to Shirley Toulson in *The Celtic Alternative*, implies "a total renunciation of familar affections and securities and a bold stepping out into the unknown." That's what my journey here to Oxford feels like, and, although it feels right that I have come here, it is a very painful experience of being cut off from loved ones back home.

What helps a bit is that I am getting to know the inhabitants of the St. Theosevia Centre, our "home away from home" for most of us. It is definitely a diverse group of personalities, religious affiliations, ages, and scholarly interests. Olivera, a Greek Orthodox from Yugoslavia, teaches at one of Oxford's colleges while she finishes research into a dissertation on child psychology. She, the only woman in our group, feels, I think, the frustration of living with all men, and has already made clear her horror at the condition certain individuals leave the kitchen. Manus, in his twenties and Irish-born, has just received his Ph.D. in engineering, and is working in that field at one of the colleges. A Roman Catholic, he receives, according to rumor, the most phone calls—next to Donald Allchin, of course. Manus's, however, are mostly from women friends. His humor is delightful, and his interest in theology and theological issues quite evident. When he discovered my interest in C. S. Lewis, he wanted to know what I thought of Lewis's *The*

Great Divorce, and when I told him that that was one book I had not read, he immediately loaned his copy to me.

Ciaran, an Irishman in his forties and Roman Catholic, is in and out, and about to leave for Scotland to visit his family before moving to Canada to join a Franciscan community. A long-time friend of Donald's when Donald was Canon Residentiary at Canterbury Cathedral, he works extensively with the gypsy (or "travelers") community, and epitomizes, I believe, the "wandering monk" of the early Celts. In fact, just looking at him and discussing with him various topics, I feel transported back into another time, the time of the Early Celtic Church—and I don't think it's only my imagination.

Peter, an Anglican in his early thirties, works at the Pusey House Library, but—I was clearly told when referring to his occupation—he is *"not* a librarian, but an archivist." Peter tends to stay more to himself, and, certainly as an Englishman, is less verbal than Manus and Ciaran. As a form of relaxation, he takes care of the backyard and garden areas—including many attempts to chase away a persistent red fox who has made his home among us. (I saw the fox this morning at breakfast as I gazed out the kitchen window, and couldn't quite believe my eyes. I had thought they only lived in the countryside, and that their main livelihood was being chased by hunters in red and black hunting uniforms!)

A Greek Orthodox American student, Saba, or Savas, is suppose to arrive soon from the States and continue his graduate studies at Pembroke College. And Donald Allchin, I was told by Olivera on the first day of my arrival, is teaching in Denmark, and won't be back for five weeks! That was disappointing news, but he left me a welcome letter in my study with a list of all sorts of people to contact for my research. If I had a year here, I don't think I could reach all of them.

Sunday, August 28

I have been crying and blowing my nose all through my writing a letter to JoAnne and the boys this morning. How I miss them! When I first started planning for this venture, it was going to be for five months; now it's four months, and it feels like forever! Before I left, I very rationally told myself that four months was really not all that much time, considering how many years I had lived alone before getting married. But there's much more to me than logic, as my crying so clearly demonstrates. I am experiencing the horrible pain of separation, and it's not that I have been gone so long (it's only been four days!), but it's looking ahead to September, October, November, December. That seems like an eternity! I must take one day at a time, and not get too caught up in looking ahead.

But I miss them so. I don't miss at all my responsibilities associated with teaching and being volunteer chair of a national lay organization, nor the busy street and noisy neighborhood that has been such a miserable part of the summer of 1988 as road crews put a new sewer system in our neighborhood, while a record-breaking heat wave and drought in the Midwest kept everyone miserable all summer. I don't even miss at this point my friends and students at the college; I mean, by the time I left St. Paul, I had really had enough of everything and everyone for awhile. I do appreciate this quiet in Oxford. It is like being on a retreat, and I am enjoying, for the most part, the relative peace and stillness of the house and of my room.

I miss my loved ones the most at certain times of day: during meals when I'm eating alone, and there's no JoAnne with whom to discuss the events of the day; at bedtime when there's no John or Daniel to wrestle or pillow-fight with or to ask me to read a book. I especially missed the three of them the other night at dinner when I found myself talking to the waiters in the Italian restaurant on the next block, just so that I had some conversation while everyone else around me was conversing with families and friends. I wanted JoAnne in particular to be there, enjoying the atmosphere and food with me, and telling me about her day. Being solitary seems more difficult when there are others having fun close by. Yes, I lived a long time alone before now, but I am just beginning to realize how strong the bonds of intimacy have been made over the years, and how the absence of my loved ones leaves a gaping hole I didn't know could exist with this intensity.

Good things are happening, though. I feel that I am meant to be here, for reasons I cannot explain as yet. In the midst of extreme loneliness, I am experiencing the profound graciousness of God, and, in the silence and solitude, an unexpected communion and solidarity.

I had dinner with the two religious writers and commentators Peter and Margaret Hebblethwaite last night and John Wilkins, the editor of *The Tablet.* I had communicated with Peter before the Synod on the Laity last fall, and tried to see him when I was in Rome, but as he wrote me later, the week I was there, he was back home, depressed at the synod's slow pace and its apparent lack of results. In his letter, however, he had invited me to visit him when I got to Oxford, so I decided to phone him when I arrived. He graciously invited me to his home for an evening meal.

Dinner was enjoyable, although I eventually found it quite difficult to follow the conversation because of my tiredness and their accents. (I know we all speak English, but theirs is a bit different than the one I'm used to.) Peter seemed disappointed with me at first when he opened the door; he may have been expecting an older man. His wife, Margaret, did not live up to my expectations. She was much younger, and did not—as I had imagined—wear long, gray hair tied neatly and tightly together in a bun. With her long, bright, almost reddish hair, I was very pleasantly surprised! Their children are most appealing, and have such strong names: Dominic, Benedict, and Cordelia.

With the children eating early and then sent to their rooms to play before bedtime (throughout the evening, I found it reassuring that their children too did not always listen to their parents!), we adults ate a leisurely meal and discussed a great variety of topics: the Synod on the Laity, the controversial *Last Temptation of Christ* movie that so many religious leaders are condemning (though most of them have never seen it themselves), Peter's work on a biography of Paul VI, and Margaret's interest in spiritual direction. Margaret does not think any spiritual directors should be paid for their work, while I suggested that lay people today, if their main source of financial support is their ministry, should be given at least some offering or stipend. (If they are hired as members of parish staffs, of course, they would not need to charge at all.) Margaret finished the evening by reading an essay from an anthology of Cardinal Gibbons's works discussing whether Catholic countries were more lax than Protestant countries in their morals because of confession and "quicky" absolution. Gibbons, of course, said not. It was getting late, and Peter noticed my tiredness, so he and John gave me a ride back to St. Theosevia's. Thank God! I don't know if I could have caught a bus at that time, or even known where to catch one.

This morning I went to Blackfriars, the residence and church of the Dominicans in Oxford, for the eucharist. I met Peter and his youngest son, Benedict, there. It was a wonderful liturgy, with many families present, a good homily, and music by a group of people with various instruments. I felt welcomed at the coffee and tea session which followed, and Peter introduced me to Peggy Loughran, a lay missionary who had just recently returned from Africa. She volunteered to take me tomorrow to John Henry Newman's Littlemore, which I've been wanting to visit since first becoming acquainted with Newman's life.

I did the grocery shopping yesterday, so I hope I have enough food to last for awhile. Am feeling more like a graduate student each day, and definitely missing JoAnne's good cooking.

Monday, August 29

Today has been rich in happenings. This morning I walked to Sr. Benedicta Ward's office at the Medieval and Renaissance Centre in downtown Oxford. I arrived tired and short of breath from the quick and long walk (I am definitely out of shape; too used to taking a car), but was filled with great anticipation. When I had first read Benedicta's book, *The Sayings of the Desert Fathers*, over ten years ago and other writings since then about those Desert Christians who acted as spiritual guides, I had felt immediately a strong sense of kinship with her, even though we had never met. When I later wrote her about some research I was having difficulty finding, she graciously responded by sending me the translation I had been looking for; and then when I began making plans for a sabbatical at Oxford, she had immediately agreed to supervise my work. All of this, of course, led me to suspect that we would get along quite well, especially because of our mutual interests in early church history and spirituality. Still, as I rang the doorbell to the center, I realized that I didn't know all that much about her, and that, really, I didn't know what to expect.

When the door swung open, I was greeted by a tall, very imposing woman dressed in the traditional habit of a nun: long flowing brown robes, a black veil, and even a white wimple! We walked up seemingly endless flights of stairs to her office, and then, after initial introductions, began to discuss our work and what I hoped to accomplish this fall. The initial awkwardness of getting to know each other was almost immediately replaced with a sense of being at ease. Benedicta seems to be a very diffident, almost shy woman, with great knowledge as well as a wonderful sense of humor. She told me she is "done" with the desert in terms of her research and writing, and is now working on a book about Bede. Seated in an old-fashioned stuffed chair and surrounded by numerous bookshelves reaching from the floor to the ceiling, I felt at home in her presence and very happy to be there. After about an hour, we set up a schedule for a series of weekly tutorials to discuss and critique my work. Benedicta suggested that I prepare something in writing each week as a basis for our discussions rather than waiting until all my research is done and only then beginning to write, as I had planned. I am looking forward to our time together this fall, and, as a result of this morning, am convinced that my plans are "on track."

This afternoon Peggy Loughran drove me to Littlemore for a tour of the Anglican parish church where John Henry Newman was first assigned, and also what came to be called "the college," which he started as an experimental community before converting to Roman Catholicism. I am now planning to stay overnight in one of the rooms which the religious community that cares for Littlemore has restored and set aside for retreatants, pilgrims, and scholars. If I can do some writing on my book, it would be appropriate to do so there, since I have admired Newman for such a long time. I consider his motto, *Cor ad cor loquitur* (heart speaks to heart), which he adopted when he became a cardinal to be the foundation of any relationship of friendship or form of spiritual mentoring.

I was struck by Littlemore's simplicity and quiet beauty, and the joy of the nun, Sr. Brigitte, who acted as our enthusiastic guide. The nuns of her community use the wooden table on which Newman wrote the book, *On the Development of Doctrine,* as their altar. This is where he met the priest who baptized him into Roman Catholicism—a joyous decision that at the same time must have also caused him so much inner conflict, knowing, as he probably did, the consternation it would cause his family and so many of his friends. He was making an especially courageous decision, considering that he was leaving everything, including Oxford, that he cherished and that was familiar to him as he moved into the totally unknown. Still, as we now know, God provided for him in so many ways that Newman could never have foreseen at the time.

The story of Newman's conversion and his lingering presence, felt especially in his private room and the chapel he designed, somehow seemed to renew my own commitment of helping in whatever way I can to transform our present church. Newman's courage—and his life—spoke to me this afternoon of persistence. His life also reminds me of the importance of developing my relationship with God, a relationship that has suffered a great deal over the past few years. With that centering, everything else loses something of its destructive impact, and life, with God's help, goes on.

Tuesday, August 30

I want to reflect upon my relationship with John and Daniel. The bookmark, "Dad," made by John and given to me before I left, reminded me this morning of my two sons who mean everything to me. In many ways, the dream of the hearth I had two years ago hit the proverbial nail on the head. It was one of those vivid dreams a person is meant to remember. In it, there are two rooms: in the first, I am with students, back in a dormitory of sorts, a big, cold room that reminds me of the prep school I attended as an adolescent and the loneliness I felt during those years. Then, in the dream, the whole place changes, and I am in a room filled with many people, even entire families, while at one end near a giant hearth a father with his family offers to share their food with me. I, however, am desperately looking for privacy at the time, and turn away from them.

At the time I interpreted the dream in terms of the polarity many people experience at midlife between separateness and intimacy, for the two rooms seemed to image so well this dichotomy and struggle in my life. As an adolescent and young adult, I had consistently searched and yearned for physical and emotional intimacy, and kept finding myself in "cold rooms" and relationships lacking warmth and depth. In my adult life, I was experiencing too much intimacy, symbolized by all the people in the second room. How to find intimacy while at the same time finding some proper boundaries was the question the dream helped me clarify.

Now I remember the words from an Hasidic saying Gretchen Berg, a friend and spiritual guide, told me and a group of lay ministers on retreat shortly after I had had that dream: "Your treasure is hidden beneath the hearth of your own home." In that context the dream makes even more sense to me now, especially the part of the father with his family. Because of so many "outside" activities, relationships, and responsibilities that have been driving me mad, I've had little energy for my own family. I haven't been able or haven't wanted to fully embrace being a parent, even though John is now seven years old and Daniel, four. Perhaps some of this resistance is related to what a former mentor of mine once told me. He said that he didn't enjoy being with his kids until they were much older, in their teens; that until then he found it difficult to relate to them. Anticipating their growing older, I think that I have unconsciously put my own children "on hold" until that day comes when we can "communicate." Ah, but Ed, that would be to miss the fun of their growing up, you fool, not to mention the harm caused by being an absent father! I am already starting to enjoy them very much, and I don't want to wait. And besides, as Gretchen's saying implied, the hearth is where I will find my real treasure....

The trip this summer to Medora in North Dakota where Teddy Roosevelt once lived, and to Mount Rushmore and the Black Hills of South Dakota was very special. I had taken John and Daniel and my parents with me, while JoAnne stayed at home so she could have some solitude before I left for Oxford. Everything was going well—until we started back! That horribly painful confrontation in the car with John and my father has taught me a great deal: how ways of relating between father and son are unconsciously passed down from one generation to another, from father to son, to father to son, to father to son, *ad infinitum,* unless somehow interrupted through the discovery of such patterns and our attempts to change them. I remember a pattern in my dad's use of anger. He would only express it when it was about to explode, and then it seemed to me, the recipient, a total rejection of oneself. I don't want to repeat that in John's and Daniel's lives. I also remember how Dad seemed to want me to be a perfect son as I was growing up. And yet on an unconscious level that is the way I was treating John on that trip: expecting him not to make mistakes even though he's only seven—as my dad evidently expected of me (and as I now expect of myself?). That is the pattern that I need to examine while I am physically away from them here in England in order to be more genuine and loving with both sons.

In some ways, like my being in England, I have to keep pinching myself to believe I'm really a parent of two smart, energetic, wonderful sons. It is what my heart always wanted and at times never thought I would have. And now that dream, that heart's desire, has become real for me, and I must no longer take it for granted, or put it (and them!) "on hold."

But I still struggle to be me, to be a good teacher as well as a good parent whose heart is fully in the task. I may simply be experiencing the old tensions which family system therapists describe as those between our need for autonomy and for community, needs that never are fully met nor are conflicts resulting from them ever fully resolved. I recognize and accept that, but I still have to acknowledge that I've given my sons and wife short shrift.

Lord, I want to be a more loving, more present parent and husband; help me to be. Help me to set aside my time-frames, goals, schedules, ideas, and simply be with John and Daniel; to listen to them, to look into their eyes, as Daniel reminds me to do. ("Come on, Daddy, look into my eyes when I'm talking to you!") Help me also to be more patient with them, especially not expressing my anger in a rejecting way that only alienates my sons from me. Not that they don't want to love me, but they cannot trust me, really, as they can their mother, because they sense (as I did with my dad) not only disapproval, but worst of all rejection, condemnation, intolerance. That distrust is what creates the behavior between us, especially John and me. Lord, please help change that. You know how much I love them and JoAnne. Thank you for their presence in my life.

Wednesday, August 31

I am back at Littlemore, settled in a tiny, yet comfortable room, and surrounded by quiet beauty and serenity. I took a taxi here this afternoon after spending the morning reading from the sayings and lives of the Desert Fathers and Mothers that Benedicta has translated. Once I had settled in here, I took a short bus ride to the Anglican Convent of the Incarnation at Fairacres where Benedicta lives. It was not at all as I had imagined. (So many of my imaginary "constructs" are proving quite inaccurate!) Even though it is a community of contemplatives, it was *not* a secluded place in the country, off Fairacre Road. No, it was right in the heart of what North Americans would call "the suburbs," easily accessible to neighbors and visitors like me. A nun in a full habit showed me around the beautiful grounds and invited me to participate in evensong at 6 P.M. So, while the community ate their dinner at 5:15, I happily browsed through their bookstore, left open with full trust that any items taken would be paid for. Again, my imagination had been off, for while I had thought that this place would have a huge bookstore, housing the Fairacre publications plus much more, it consisted only of one small room with tiny pamphlets and booklets on various shelves in no particular order. Still, I gratefully bought a number of their pamphlets, and then joined the community for prayer.

As in St. Theosevia's front hallway, the convent's chapel has the famous Rublev icon of the Holy Trinity over its main altar. Listening to the Divine Office sung by the community made me aware of my own longing to pray, to discover new ways of praying, to express my own "great yearning," as Abraham Joshua Heschel says, "that sweeps eternity: the yearning to praise, the yearning to serve." My soul seeks times of quiet as well as a community of some kind in which to pray. I had been hoping that the St. Theosevia Centre would provide that opportunity, and Donald Allchin had mentioned it as a possibility, but evidently communal prayer has not occurred, possibly due to the great diversity of religious backgrounds and professional interests of the inhabitants; perhaps more likely because of our diverse work and study schedules. I hope something along that line will yet develop while I am here in Oxford, and, if we can't pray together in the house, then I will go to where some of the house members pray.

I returned by bus to Littlemore after the evening prayer, and had a dinner of steak and chips and peas (the English seem to include the latter in almost every meal!). I ate across the street at the pub in what the owners call, "the Cardinal's study," the place where Newman supposedly dined. Of course, I wished that JoAnne was there, but I managed to take in the environment without a great deal of regret. As Roland Walls says in a pamphlet entitled *From Loneliness to Solitude* that I picked up at Fairacres, "at moments you find you can really notice things. When you are alone, books, food, music, the weather, the odd sparrow, take on a sharper edge, a quality, a presence that goes unnoticed when company is there. I am able to live more intensely in the middle of the miracle of the existence of things."

Thus far, my time away is definitely becoming a journey into solitude, and I haven't even been here a week. So much in one week of quiet and aloneness, with my soul drinking deeply, and often painfully, of those realities. Yet, I have noticed in myself and in my prayers a greater awareness of those who are suffering (from the bus driver with his many stops to the elderly woman attempting to cross the street), and a greater sense of solidarity with them than before when I was so preoccupied with the business and busy-ness of living.

I find myself thinking more about the reality of the soul. "Soul" is a part of contemporary language and culture, though we seldom think of what we mean when we use that term: soul-searching, soul food, soul brother (from the American black culture of the 1960s), soul music, soul mates, and, for the Celts, soul friends. My own understanding of the soul has been helped a great deal by Carl Jung's description of it. After years of clinical work, he came to the conclusion that it is composed, as is our physical make-up, of individual elements which were all already present in our ancestors, and that these ancestral components are only partially at home with what is new, with our contemporary age. The line by him which comes back to me, one to which I frequently refer in my classes: "We are very far from having finished completely with the Middle Ages, classical antiquity, and primitivity, as our modern psyches pretend."

That quotation seems very important to me, for Jung implies that the more we know and have studied history, the more we will understand ourselves, since that history still lives in us, not only on a cultural level, but very much in our personal lives on an unconscious level. At the same time Jung warns us in somewhat apocalyptic imagery and tone about the ever-wider violence that can result when we live too much in the future, disconnected from our roots. He says that it is precisely the loss of connection with the past, our uprootedness, which has given rise to the deep dissatisfaction and unhappiness of modern civilization, to what he calls the "flurry and haste" of modern life. The less we understand of our fathers and forefathers, he says (I would add "mothers and foremothers"), the less we understand ourselves.

Thus the reason why more people today, myself included, search for ancestral and spiritual roots: our souls yearn for connections, communion with a deeper reality than what our culture offers us. We yearn for sources that will put us in touch with our deeper selves, and, perhaps most of all, with our God. This communion can only happen with our relating within time to time itself, and rather than only focusing on our future we need to begin with the relationship of our past (often present on an unconscious level) with the present, our contemporary world.

Our North American culture, however, consistently values the opposite of what Jung is advocating in his writings. Constantly, it seems, American advertizing and politics hold out ephemeral promises that utopia is just around the corner; that we are getting better and better because of our technology; or that the ever-changing New is where happiness can be found. Yet that reliance on the future and on technological products and gadgets to make our futures bright and "safe," Jung seems to warn, only leads to greater violence: not only the violence the poor and hungry in our midst experience as the result of our negligence, but the loss of our own humanity as we become increasingly anxious about our security and selfish about gaining "success." The more we concentrate solely upon "getting ahead," the more those new forms of addiction seem to lead us to greater unhappiness, and eventually greater despair of soul, both collective and personal.

What is especially worthwhile about Jung is his description of the "loss of soul." He equates that loss with our being cut off from the life of the feminine and the unconscious, as well as from our roots, our pasts, or what he describes as the mythic "land of our ancestors." The very definition of it tells us a great deal inversely how we would begin to find our souls: by paying attention to the feminine and the unconscious, our roots, our pasts, and especially the "ancestral components" that dwell within.

The journey here to Oxford does have much to do with the soul, my soul. Since Grandma Mary's death, I have been wanting to learn more about the soul's reality, and in particular to discern more about my soul's inheritance. I need to understand more about "soul" if I am to write on what it means to be a soul friend. So I have quite literally come to the land of my ancestors, and this fall will be researching the history of those Celtic lands and their spiritual heritage. Discovering more of that history and finding my own soul, I think, is intimately linked with my emerging self.

The Celtic figure in my dreams whom I now call "Cuthbert" (after the saint of Lindisfarne) came at the right time, for in the midst of great personal confusion and unhappiness he pointed out a new direction in my life. He helped me become aware of my need to follow my own heart in my teaching and my own voice in my writing without succumbing to others' expectations. As I continue to try to understand the various layers of meaning the dream of Cuthbert holds, he has become an important inner guide. Like Jung's Philemon, the dream figure that came to Jung at midlife, Cuthbert seems to hold secrets that lie in the depth of my soul.

How else to explain the dream I had this past spring on March 20, Cuthbert's feast day, the unusually long and vivid one that I mysteriously kept re-entering despite different times of waking up during the night? I haven't forgotten its plot and characters. It opens with a group of people having a workshop or involved in a course in a big, old brick building. A storm comes up suddenly, with two or three tornadoes, and we run for cover. Some head for rs and climb into them for protection. I and a few others stay inside. My Grandma Mary is with us, I discover with great surprise, an old, thin, wan-looking woman I barely recognize. As parts of the building begin to collapse, I help her onto the second floor and leave her pressed against a wall, and then run for cover with John and Daniel to the basement. I feel guilty at having left her there alone, and frightened for her safety, and wonder why I didn't bring her with me!

Somehow the storm subsides, and we survivors gather again. I begin to walk through the building, forgetting about Grandma Mary or presuming that she is no longer alive. Then I hear her breathing—an unpleasant rasping sound, yet strong—and I spy her among the fallen bricks. I go to her, and we cry tears of joy. She's still alive; hurt, but okay! She is bleeding from the falling bricks, and I help dig her out and begin to bind up her legs so that she can walk again. Later in the dream, I find myself teaching a course on ecclesiology in what's left standing of the building. Each of us survivors tells the story of how we survived the storm, and, in answer to a question about the church, I say that this happening to us is precisely what the church is about: beginning with something seemingly solid and indestructible, we find ourselves in the midst of life's storms, and then, with our "security" gone, we tell our stories of survival to each other, and realize in the telling that God has always been there. "That," I tell the students, "is what church is all about."

I remember awaking from the dream with a great sense of inner peace and serenity, and am immediately aware that it probably contained many layers of meaning. The storm surely is a symbol of where my life was at that time. That I and my sons (symbols of my generativity and future hopes) survive by going into the basement (the depths) also offers great hope. And the figure of my grandmother provides, I think, intimations of an emerging life-task: to recover the Celtic spiritual heritage which is mine, and, along with others, to bring it out of the ruins of neglect so that it can walk again.

According to Gretchen whom I went to see after having this dream, the grandmother figure coincides with the traditional portrayal of Ireland as a woman, and the equating of wisdom itself with the feminine. It may be, since Grandma Mary appears so wan and emaciated in the dream, that I need, Gretchen said, to pay more attention to my spiritual heritage—and to my creative side. That Grandma Mary and I survive the storm may also carry the message that I need to learn to trust more (as Grandma always did when she was physically alive) that somehow all will be well. Gretchen was quite pointed about this. She said that tornadoes, while they can be destructive, are really only blowing air, air without substance; and the dream finds me still alive, despite some of the destruction they have caused. More than that, I am not "merely alive," but changed profoundly by my having gone through the storm itself. This, she said, was a hopeful message from the unconscious. She also told me to remember the story from Scriptures in Matthew 8: when Jesus is out on the lake and a storm comes up. What does he do? He faces the storm, and he tells those who are in the boat with him, "Why are you so frightened, you of little faith?"

It is good to be here in Newman's sacred space, and to be sleeping tonight in the same room where Fr. Barberi slept, sheltered from the storm and rain outside, the night Newman requested from him admission to Catholicism. I prayed tonight to John Henry Newman for peace of heart, and for the ability to work within the church at a time when I still feel so alienated from it.

❉ 2 ❉

HEART SPEAKS TO HEART
September 1-13, 1988

When I was abroad, the sight of so many great places, venerable shrines, and noble churches, much impressed my imagination.
And my heart was touched also.

John Henry Newman, *Apologia pro Vita Sua*

Thursday, September 1

I have decided to stay two more days here at Littlemore, since it is turning out to be a very quiet place for research and reflection. I had thought that perhaps with tourists and Newman devotees there would be too many interruptions, but such is not the case. Sr. Brigette has made me feel most welcome, and at her invitation I joined her community in evening prayer last night. Later in the evening I listened to the recording of "The Dream of Gerontius" that she loaned me, the dramatic poem written by Newman in his old age. Set to music, it dramatically portrays the death of an old man and what happens to his soul as he enters into eternity. Waking this morning and sitting quietly by myself while eating a simple breakfast of cereal and toast, I thought of the line from his poetry: "This silence pours a solitariness into the very essence of my soul." For some reason I thought of my visit the previous summer to Norwich and the cell of Julian, the fourteenth-century English mystic.

The patristics conference at Oxford was over, and I had a few days before returning home. A colleague and I had gone back to London, and while he decided to stay in the city, I wanted to see Norwich. I got up early Sunday morning, took the subway to Paddington Station, and then a train to Norwich from there. Although the train was delayed several hours, once I boarded it the trip itself was most pleasant. My only fear, since it was Sunday and I knew I wouldn't arrive in the city until early afternoon, was that Julian's church might be closed. That fear was unfounded. I found the church quite easily with the help of a friendly man at the station. There it was on a beautiful sunny afternoon, located off the beaten-trail, in a commercial part of the city near the river, with its doors open to traveling pilgrims like myself who arrive at odd hours. I went immediately to Julian's cell, located inside, and was pleased to see that I would have it for myself, since there were no other visitors around.

I found myself once again in a spot made holy by the presence of a wisdom figure whose writings have taught me so much about the motherhood of God and the serenity that is found in God's loving embrace. I prayed silently to her that day, thanking her for the gift of her revelations. Then I turned to the window where she had once counseled people like Margery Kempe from right off the street. Even though Julian's original cell and church were destroyed by falling bombs during World War II, this was her sacred space, and I imagined how she had centered her life in God here, and how she had expressed this new centering in the ministry of spiritual guidance. As I left, I lit a candle outside the door of the cell for a safe trip home, and another for Julian's continued guidance in my life. Like my experience here this morning living in Newman's sacred space, my visit to Norwich will always be remembered, for some sort of intimacy seems to be mysteriously established with the saints whenever we go to their shrines. Their lives may have preceded ours by years and even centuries, yet somehow they're very much interconnected with ours.

What now strikes me about my visit to Julian's shrine is that she had two windows in her cell of solitude: one to the sanctuary of the church in which she had been enclosed, and one to the busy world outside. The first window she opened in order to pray with the eucharistic community and receive Holy Communion from the priest; the second window she opened to a busy thoroughfare in order to listen to those who came to her for spiritual advice. Those two windows, I think, symbolize the two aspects of the spiritual life: 1) our need to cultivate a relationship of intimacy with God, the source of our lives, and, 2) our need to strengthen our solidarity—through our ministries—with all of humanity, our brothers and sisters in the flesh.

Spiritual guidance, I am coming to see, is concerned with the entire person (body and soul, emotion, and intellect) in relationship with God. Unlike pastoral or psychological counseling, it is not primarily focused upon a specific crisis or an emotional problem, yet it will not exclude those "ordinary" aspects of life when they occur. For those involved in that ministry of spiritual guidance, one's competence can be strengthened through a formation program which invites familiarity with theological reflection, Scripture, and the history of Judeo-Christian spirituality. The heart of this ministry, however, is the spiritual guide's own self-knowledge and relationship with God. That "ground" or soil is nourished through prayer, a life of prayer that inexplicably seems to lead us again and again (when we forget) not only to the discovery of God's goodness, but to the acknowledgment of our own human limitations and of our propensity to sin. Being aware of this propensity is, as Thomas Merton says so well, "the beginning of wisdom." It teaches us about our need for God in our lives, and for one another, and, perhaps closely tied in with that, our ongoing need for reconciliation...day after day after day.

That is one characteristic of the early Celtic churches that does not seem to be discussed all that much in what I have been able to find thusfar in my research: the awareness they had as Christian communities of the destructive power of sin, and, as a corollary, the recognition of their need for seeking forgiveness. Their history is certainly filled with stories of sinful deeds; about lay people, for example, in charge of the later monasteries who plundered other monasteries out of greed or a thirst for revenge. It also contains the stories of being sinned against by others, including those Viking raiders who came to their lands, pillaged the countryside, and destroyed the places made holy by the lives and ministries of the saints. We can admire certain qualities of the early Christian Celts and look to them for what they can teach us today about Christian spirituality and the ministry of spiritual guidance, but it is important not to over-romanticize them or the early church of which they were a part. That would be unfair to them and their own call to holiness. Their lives, like ours, were filled with conflict and struggle; they too attempted to live according to the gospels, but at the same time they experienced uncertainties and life-patterns that seemed so intractable; they too lived with indecision and lack of clarity in doing what is best. That is why the ministry of the *anamchara*, or soul friend, grew quickly in the Celtic lands: precisely because people realized their need for help in discerning what God was asking of them and the need to acknowledge the powerful, destructive patterns of sin. When we look at the lives of certain Celtic wisdom figures, we discover this. The great St. Columcille, for example, only began his ministry of evangelization to Scotland in the sixth century because of the strife, according to legend, brought about by his stubbornness, his repentance and confession to his *anamchara*, and that *anamchara's* spiritual advice that he go into exile to make restitution for his sins.

The early Christian Celts, besides being creative people with riotous imaginations (a quality clearly reflected in the beauty and story-telling of the illuminated manuscripts, such as the *Book of Kells*, the *Lindisfarne Gospels*, and the *Book of Durrow*) were also mature people, aware of their temptations to abuse their power and gifts, and of their ability to hurt grievously those whom they loved the most. They were conscious of these dimensions because in their own lives they had done so, and could quite easily do so again. That is why they turned to the soul friends, for they realized any reconciliation or "success" in attempting to deal with the powerful reality of sin would only come through God's help. From their own experiences, the healing power of their God was so often mediated through the compassionate presence of a soul friend: someone with whom we can speak openly and honestly in the language of the heart.

Christ, according to St. Augustine, is the hidden teacher of the heart. He is our "companion" on the journey of our lives, a word that comes from the Latin, *cum* (with) *panis* (bread). A person who shares bread, life, a meal with us becomes, through our sharing with him or her, what the Christian Celts called a soul friend. Through a person's friendship and loving acceptance of us, we find nourishment and sustenance for our pilgrimage through time. Soul friendship is an intimate, deeply caring relationship in which sins can be acknowledged openly, where God's goodness and forgiveness are affirmed, and where we can discern the movements of our hearts. In the Celtic churches, everyone was expected to have a soul friend, for, as Brigit said once to a cleric who came to her for spiritual guidance, "Anyone without a soul friend is like a body without a head; like a limey well, not good for wishing."

4 P.M.

I took a walk around the neighborhood to clear my mind after a full day of reading, and stopped for a cup of coffee at a nearby store before returning here to my desk. While I have been trying to be attentive to the books I brought with me to read, on another level I often find my concentration interrupted. What is it; what's going on?

I am haunted with feelings of guilt in how I treated my son, John, on the trip this summer to his grandparents' house, to Medora, to the Black Hills and back, before I left. How he does seem to constellate my dark side, my shadow! My parenting of him gets mixed in, I think, with the parenting I received.

There we were on our way back from the Black Hills, all five of us (Mom, Dad, John, Daniel, and myself) crammed into the car for almost the entire day, getting increasingly tired and on each other's nerves, as I tried to "make time" in order to reach my parents' house before midnight. Then it happened. We'd left the pizza place where we had eaten our supper, and about ten minutes out of a little town in South Dakota, John asked where the canteen was that I had given him as a souvenir of our trip. When none of us could find the canteen, it became apparent that it had been left behind. I immediately blamed John, and became angry not only for this oversight on his part, but for others on the trip. (And, of course, the canteen had been a gift from me....) As I turned the car around, I kept berating him until he blurted out, "That hurts—you're hurting me," and began to cry. My Dad sat there quietly—ominously, I thought—and then asked if I wanted his opinion on the subject. "No," I snapped defensively, "stay out of it." Following that response, the silence in the car was deafening.

After I'd driven back to the restaurant and picked up the canteen, Dad exploded, "You don't have to treat him that way! What kind of example are you giving?" I replied instantly, enraged and threatened by his outburst, "Stay out of it, and don't correct me in front of my sons!" He yelled back, "I will never go on a trip with you again; all we ever do is fight!"

I drove on, still angry at John and now at my father, tired from all the driving, feeling guilty about our exchange, and especially hurt at his words about never going on a trip with me again. Although at that moment I didn't ever want another trip with him, I thought his remarks were uncalled for, and they brought back those memories of other conflicts with him earlier in my life. "You hurt me," I said. "I was the one who had suggested this trip; I was the one who wanted to spend more time with you and Mom, and it really has been a good trip up until now!"

Then, convinced that he was once again over-reacting (as I

remembered him doing when I was growing up) and being unfair, I decided I would not say another word.

By this time, the only sounds in the car were John's muffled sobs
(I had ended the entire "discussion" by peevishly telling him, "I
hope you're satisfied"), as well as Mom's crying. Daniel didn't help
matters any when he got the last word in, "You made Grandma
cry." As we drove on through the darkness in a car that had become
suddenly uncomfortably small, something began to work its way
through my anger and hurt into my consciousness. I came to the
realization that even though I was tired, I had set myself up for all
of that by over-reacting to John first, and then over-reacting to Dad
by telling him in effect to shut up and stay out of it. Then, as time
passed, yet another painful insight pressed itself through my wall
of defensiveness: that maybe both my son and father had been tired
too, and thus not fully responsible for their actions of forgetfulness
and outrage. Later, it became clear to me how much I loved them
both and how much each meant to me. My increasing awareness
at midlife that our days and years are not limitless was why I had
arranged this trip; that was why I wanted to spend more time
with them, and for them to spend more time with each other.

My earlier words of Dad's hurting me and the silence in the car
for the rest of the trip evidently had their own effect on Dad, too.
By the time we reached my parents' house, he was apologizing to
me, as I was to him, and to my sleepy son John, awakened by our
arrival and, for the most part, unable to comprehend what was
going on!

The next day, another insight helped clarify why I felt not only
guilty and ashamed at my behavior the previous night toward
both my father and my son, but also puzzled by the anger that
had possessed me. I was telling Mom how the conflict between
John and me and its unexpected aftermath had made me painfully aware that I consistently treat John as if he were much older, as
if he shouldn't make mistakes at all. She immediately responded,
"Well, that's how your father always treated you, as much as I
tried to tell him that you were only a child!" When she said that,

something deep within me clicked, and I recognized then how I had unconsciously fallen into a pattern which had been inherited.

This new awareness has not taken away the guilt and lingering self-hatred for what happened in the car that night, but it has paradoxically led to a sense of liberation. It wasn't that, in retaliation, I wanted to blame Dad yet again for something wrong with me. No, now that I have found the origins of the pattern of my relating to my oldest son, I no longer have to let it control me unconsciously and with such destructive results. That pattern, of course, is well-established and its origins may go back generations, possibly passed on from my paternal grandfather to my father and on to me. With such deep rootedness, it may not—probably will not—go away. But, as a result of my mother's words, I have been given a better handle on future ways of behaving toward my sons and father, too. And, perhaps, with God's help, that pattern may not have to become so deeply ingrained in either John or Daniel.

My guilt remains, but because of that trip and what it taught me I want to get more in touch with my unconscious expectations of myself, of my parents, of my sons. Those expectations are what I must continue to look at while I am away if I am ever to be more compassionate and especially forgiving of those I love—and of myself.

My rage at John for making mistakes that any child or any adult might make, my unreasonableness, vindictiveness, and rejection of him: those are characteristics of my shadow side. They reflect my own perfectionistic demands toward myself and the self-rejection that necessarily follows when I am unable to live up to those unrealistic expectations. The ways I have failed to have compassion for myself as a child and on through my adolescent and adult years are the ways that I have been treating John. Daniel I get angry with and then forget it; John, my first born, I want to be the perfect son. He is like me: his sensitivity, his creativity, his ability to make friends; yes, most of all, his wanting his father to love him.

I do love him, a deep, deep love that cannot be put into words, as I love my second-born, Daniel, who asks me, "Who do you love more, John or me?" And I can only reply truthfully, "Daniel, I love you both with all my heart; there's no room to love either of you less—or more."

Part of my feelings of loneliness this past week in England are connected, I think, with guilt and fear: guilt that I am gone from my family for so long and that JoAnne must bear the brunt of my decision to come here; fear that my children in my absence will conclude that I don't love them or care for them anymore. What I tried to convey to JoAnne before I left was that I believe strongly, for some inexplicable reason, that I had to come here; that coming here when I did was as important as my going into clinical training with alcoholics and my pursuing graduate studies in the 1970s. Now that I'm here, I still don't fully understand why, but I know that it's more than research purposes that have drawn me. I only pray that she and John and Daniel will someday understand, as I continue to hope that my pilgrimage away from them will benefit others, especially my two sons.

My dark side. Solitude is bringing out so much in me. Yes, I have begun to experience new levels of compassion for others as I face my own loneliness. But I am also encountering the demons of self-hatred and disgust, of guilt, and fear, and shame.

Lord, accept my life into your hands; teach me wisdom and especially compassion. Help me become more fully aware of when the shadow of rejection, judgment, rage is constellated, especially with my loved ones, in this case, with John. Somehow I know now that rage toward him originates in the wounds of my own childhood. Granted, some of my impatient reaction might be primordial; that is, something lying deep within the psyche, learned when fathers in the wilderness or jungle could not allow their sons to make mistakes that might cost them their lives. Still, much of it may be simply (!) rooted in my not allowing those I love to be themselves, to be human, to have limitations, to make mistakes, because I do not allow myself to have or make them.

Paradoxically, much of my reaction may even find its origin in my care, my love. If I didn't love John as much as I do, I wouldn't feel so intensely about him, and experience such angry and hurt feelings at times, as well as experience so intensely my present guilt. But I am an adult, and I need to consciously learn ways of expressing anger that do not violate a young boy's spirit and trust.

In retrospect, I see now how John has also been my teacher. When he cried out that he was "hurting" at my continued ranting at his mistake in forgetting the canteen, he unwittingly taught me of my need to tell my father when his words had hurt me. My deeply-entrenched pattern for so many years had been to bury the feelings, not acknowlege the pain, and thus grow ever more distant from Dad as both of us grew older. Good for John!

Friday, September 2

I bought some books about Newman that were for sale in the library here at Littlemore, and have been glancing through them when not doing my other research and writing. For a long time I have admired and respected this man who is now being considered for sainthood, and have enjoyed teaching about him in various courses. When I went to Rome at the time of the Synod on the Laity (almost a year ago now), I took his book with me, *On Consulting the Faithful in Matters of Doctrine*, and read it on the plane. What he wrote was so theologically sound, and that was what I found so exciting and exhilarating then: that in preparation for the synod and the pope's coming to the United States for a pastoral visit last fall, we laypeople had been consulted. Many of us hoped, I think, that all of this consultation would somehow have a positive effect on the life of the world-church. After returning to the States, however, and reading in the papers how little, if anything, would change, the words of Newman in the conclusion of that book came back to me. He warned, years ahead of Vatican II, that when laypeople are cut off from important issues of church life, "the educated classes will terminate in indifference" and "the poorer in superstition." The Synod on the Laity, I thought, had all the potential for being significant, but instead of the openness with which it began, there seems to have followed only secrecy and platitudes. What I am most afraid of is that educated Roman Catholics, especially women and young people, may increasingly become indifferent to an apparently uncaring institutional church. That indifference, as well as the increase of superstition, will make us all the poorer. I don't want to see the church in the United States go the way of France, practically wiped out for generations, or even of Italy, where the churches are for the most part beautiful tourist attractions, but the eucharist itself mainly the domain of older women and aging clerics.

Being here with Newman, however, has reminded me of the struggles he had to put up with in his own day. I am also reminded of why his writings have had such a powerful effect on people like myself. "A great author," according to him, "is not just someone who has splendid phrases and is a dealer in words; he is one who has his great or rich visions before him, has something to say and knows how to say it—this is his characteristic and personal gift.... Yet all the time he has with him the charm of simplicity, an incommunicable plainness." An article Sr. Brigette gave me by Elizabeth Stopp in the newsletter put out by "the Friends of Cardinal Newman" says that Newman's writing was "essentially pastoral, for souls, for individuals," and "writing of this kind is always, according to Newman, of a personal character." I think that personal approach is why so many people have come to identify with him, and, most of all, love him as they would a close friend.

I am very impressed with the religious community called "The Work" which is now in charge of Littlemore. The foundress, Sr. Brigitte told me, was Julia Verhaeghe, a Belgian, whose precarious health evidently did not get in the way of her making a significant contribution to the life of the church. Dedicated to Christian unity, especially within the Roman Catholic church, "The Work" now has centers in many other European countries, as well as Israel and Africa. Most surprisingly, its membership is not limited to only priests or vowed religious, but includes bishops, seminarians, and even families and individual lay people in a way that is adapted to each state of life. The spirituality of "The Work" originates, Sister Brigitte tells me, in Mother Julia's early affection for the writings of St. Paul and, later, in her reading a book by John Henry Newman with whom she discovered a spiritual kinship. Now "The Work," besides being involved in a great variety of ministries, is sponsoring symposia and facilitating scholarship on Newman, and actively promoting his canonization. Sr. Brigitte, herself a scholar in philosophy, embodies much of that enthusiasm for Newman, and I appreciate her generosity and hospitality.

I am fascinated with Newman's original idea of starting a small community here at Littlemore. Evidently, it came from his reading of the Desert Fathers (which is what I am now doing with Benedicta), and his own desire to find some form of "cell" for solitude from his pastoral and academic responsibilities. He did not want to be entirely alone, and decided, like the early desert hermits, to bring together a few friends who could pursue their scholarship and spirituality together. As Newman wrote, "as I made Littlemore a place of retirement for myself, so did I offer it to others."

I hate to leave this place. Its quiet solitude and peaceful environment have positively affected my research and writing—and personal reflection. But a BBC television crew is coming to film a program on Newman later this afternoon, and I want to get back to St. Theosevia's.

Sunday, September 4

I had a long talk with JoAnne and the boys on the phone this afternoon. The time difference of six hours makes it difficult for us to communicate with each other, since when they are just awakening, it is the middle of the afternoon here. I noticed immediately that JoAnne's voice seemed strained, and then she told me that her paternal grandmother, Grandma Roban, died unexpectedly last Wednesday. I can't believe it! I just assumed when I left that I would see her again; that she would be a part of our lives for some years.

I miss her already. She could be so cantankerous, especially as she got older and experienced all the limitations that age can bring, but she was special to me. From the time she and I first met when I was dating JoAnne, I had the feeling that she loved me and wanted JoAnne's and my relationship to work out. Her last words to me before I left for Oxford, after she'd taken all of us out for dinner, were typical of her blunt honesty: "If you have any temptations while you're gone, just think of me, an ugly, old woman."

I grieve her passing, especially because I wasn't there for JoAnne when she and the boys needed me. I deeply regret that.

Grandma Roban's death, my grief and regret and guilt at being gone, my missing JoAnne and the boys so much—all came together in my tears over the phone. I couldn't help them. I didn't want to cry; I wanted to be strong for them. Daniel picked up the phone and started jabbering immediately, "Do you know what...?" And then, hearing me crying, he stopped talking and asked me if I was sad, and when I said yes—through my tears—he started crying too. Then John came on, John, the friendly, quiet one on the other end of the line so many miles away. "Still waters run deep," just like his Dad. After hanging up, I felt so powerless and so depressed.

Today was a full day, besides that phone call. I went to Blackfriars for Mass this morning, did the laundry in the nearby laundromat (with its helpful "Just follow the easy directions on the machine"—they weren't that easy!), and spent the entire afternoon reading about the desert fathers and mothers. This evening I went with Olivera and Savas to the St. Giles Fair, a holdover from medieval times. There was a special opening prayer service with a choir, some robed Anglican priests, and members of the Town Council all assembled on a huge, gold merry-go-round. Our singing was accompanied by the calliope located on it, and it seemed a bit of a time-warp and culture-shock to be singing such songs as "Onward Christian Soldiers" and "God Save the Queen." Beautiful! Savas, who arrived yesterday at St. Theosevia's, invited me to dinner at an Indian restaurant following the service, and even paid for my dinner because, he said, "You're new to Oxford, and I want you to feel welcome." (This gesture of hospitality, of course, has now made him a friend for life.) He and I have a great deal in common regarding political views, historical, literary, and theological interests, and life goals. I think our friendship will grow. It's as if I have known him many years already.

Bless him, Lord, and all those who are sheltered in this house, and my family so far away from me. And may Grandma Roban rest in peace.

Monday, September 5

I want to record a wisdom saying attributed to Abba Nilus from Benedicta's *The Desert of the Heart,* a book that contains stories from the early desert fathers and mothers. It has spoken directly to me this morning during my time of prayer: "Prayer is the seed of gentleness and the absence of anger."

Something of a pattern is emerging in my daily routine: before I get started on my research each morning, I begin my day with prayer. Increasingly aware of my need for "visuals" and symbols for praying, I have set up a small shrine on my desk near the window overlooking the garden. It consists of the miniature icon of Jesus which I brought with me from home, and a votive candle which I bought in Oxford. I light the candle before beginning my prayer. Gretchen Berg taught me that: how lighting a candle can help us dispel all the distractions we bring to our prayer, and create an atmosphere of quiet meditation. Now when I light the candle before my shrine, I consciously place myself in God's loving presence, and then, through a series of deep breaths, begin to empty myself of everything that gets in the way of my communing with God. As I breathe, I offer up my concerns to the Holy

One, and then listen to what the silence reveals. Sometimes I just sit there quietly; other times I read slowly and reflectively from a book. This simple method seems to work for me, and through it I am beginning to experience more of the gentleness that the desert father, Nilus, talks about, as well as what seems to be an inner stirring within, a repentance of some kind: a lightening, a gradual change of heart.

Yesterday was another wonderfully rich day in Oxford. It started with my meeting Benedicta at the Bodleian Library and going through the procedures there of gaining admittance to one of the most prestigious libraries in the world. After the paperwork and picture-taking session, I sat down with a man dressed in academic robes and took a formal oath to abide by the rules of the library: no smoking, no stealing, no desecration of property. When that rather solemn exercise was over, I joined Benedicta at the Medieval and Renaissance Centre for a fascinating tutorial on the desert monastic tradition. She gave me a good number of suggestions about resources that might be helpful for my writing, and made various comments about spiritual direction as practiced among the Desert Christians of the fourth century. As we talked, I was struck by the vast amount of knowledge she obviously has. But another awareness came to me. She is not a tall woman, or large, as I had originally perceived her. She is about my height. I can only conclude that it was my projections of her international reputation for scholarship and my great respect for her that "enlarged" her in my eyes beyond her physical stature. Interesting psychological note! How often perhaps we distort people due to our expectations, or worse, our prejudices.

After our meeting, I went to the lecture hall just down the steps from her office. The topic of her lecture was the Middle Ages, a period with which she is very familiar. I thoroughly enjoyed the way she skillfully wove together examples from art, literature, poetry, and religion into her historical introduction. The lecture was given to a group of American college students studying here this fall. After Benedicta's presentation, I met some of them, including a few from Minnesota who were from Carleton College and St. Cloud State. They seemed as excited as I was to actually be living in Oxford, but at the same time, behind the smiles, I perceived some of the same anxiety and loneliness at being away from family and friends. When I left the center, I went to the restaurant at St. Aldgate's, across from Christ Church, and had lunch with a friendly couple I had never met before. (The English have this custom of joining you at table if there are no open spots elsewhere.)

Following that enjoyable exchange with total strangers, I went on to the University Chapel, St. Mary's, for an organ concert from the compositions of Samuel Wesley, Thomas Tomkins, and Mozart. Somewhere I had picked up a brochure advertizing this series of musical concerts being offered each Monday this fall at lunchtime. What an opportunity to relax a little and enjoy the music before getting down to work. I loved being in that old church, now filled with sunlight and music, and looking up at the large, ornate pulpit where C. S. Lewis, John Henry Newman, John Wesley, and other notables had once preached.

When the concert had concluded, I left St. Mary's and walked a short distance (just behind it) and entered what I had come to consider the "holy of holies," the Bodleian. For years I had wanted to enter its sacred precincts, and now at last I had access to its vast collection of books, containing the wisdom of centuries. Entering, I soon discovered, was the easy part, as I attempted (with the help of a very patient librarian) to learn the system of classification and retrieval of books. Here a person cannot check anything out, but must first locate the reference in a labyrinth of books located on various shelves, and then fill out a special form in order to (eventually) receive the book one desires to use.

While I waited for my first book (I was told it sometimes takes hours), I walked across the yard and up the steps to the Radcliffe Camera, one of the most imposing buildings at Oxford, located on a large expanse of grass and surrounded by the walls of adjoining colleges. Again, I felt as if I were entering a sacred temple. After quickly getting some sense of direction and familiarity with the place (the men's toilet, for example, is called "the men's cloak-room"—an interesting euphemism), I went to the theology section downstairs. There, almost immediately, I discovered on the shelf a book by Nora Chadwick, *The Age of the Saints in the Early Celtic Church*, for which I had been searching for years. I perused its pages, and also "ordered up" (as they say) a book by her on the druids that would help me with my research.

Before getting back to St. Theosevia's later that afternoon, I had to "run the gauntlet" as I attempted to get through the thousands of people at the St. Giles Fair. I succeeded (very slowly), and then cooked supper—blood sausage I had purchased earlier. Everyone else in the kitchen seemed totally disgusted with it, and no one would accept my offer to share it, although Manus finally did. (Of course, considering what I've seen him usually prepare, he is, like me, not all that discriminating.) This was the first time all of us at St. Theosevia's were together since I arrived, each of us making our own supper in the crowded kitchen space—and it was fun. Somehow we got on the subject of apparitions, myrrh-smelling statues, and other non-rational phenomena. This is an interesting side of religion that many academics totally discredit, while so many people flock to swaying statues in Ireland and apparitions of Mary in Yugoslavia. We didn't reach any conclusions among ourselves, but the discussion, like that with Benedicta in the morning, was most intriguing, providing further food for thought. Thank you, Lord, for such a great wealth of personali-ties, religious traditions, and theological views, all of which reside under one roof and one God.

Tuesday, September 6

This morning I read from Benedicta's *Lives of the Desert Fathers* and her new book, *Harlots of the Desert*. I am beginning to see the two spiritual traditions, that of the desert and of the Celtic, as hav-ing much in common. Both of them highly valued the tradition of spiritual mentoring as a resource for their spiritual development;

both connected their daily work with prayer; both traditions too led very simple lifestyles in communion with the natural elements. I want to do more research and writing in that area, and would like to teach a course on those two traditions when I get back to the States.

This afternoon I took a bus over Magdalen bridge and back to the Convent of the Incarnation at Fairacres. On my first brief visit there a week ago, I arranged to meet with a Sr. Helen Columba, someone whom Dolores Leckey suggested I see. Sr. Columba and I hit it off immediately when we were introduced, especially when she told me how she too had been influenced by unexpected dreams in her forties, while living on Iona. She said that going to that holy place had changed her life dramatically, and she described how on her first visit she had a sense of having been there before, as I had at Glendalough the first time I visited Ireland. Then she said out of the blue, "Perhaps your time here in Oxford will have a significant effect on you in some ways you have yet to discover." At her words I felt a deep resonance within, as if she had physically struck me. On one level, I sensed a resounding "yes"; at a more rational level, I heard myself ask the question (without speaking it aloud), "But how?"

We went on to discuss various characteristics of Celtic spirituality that we had both identified over the years, but as we talked I began to realize how much of that spirituality already lives in me—has lived in me for years at the core of my being. I share with those ancestral figures a strong sense of the presence of God in nature, a concern for the unfortunate and for social justice, a deep feeling of linkage with the communion of saints, love and appreciation for one's family and friends, and (as I have experienced already) deep affection and longing for hearth and home that struggles with a kind of wanderlust (the desire to travel and visit foreign shores). Sr. Columba also mentioned one other characteristic which I had never heard before.

"The Celtic people," she said, "are a people of extremes."

"What do you mean?" I asked. "I've never read about that or heard it articulated."

"Well," she said, "they seem to have two sides to them that are felt and manifest in sometimes extreme and dramatically different ways. When they are happy, happiness and joy are overflowing, expressed in music, dance, fellowship, and merriment; when they are sad or melancholy, those emotions too are just as deeply felt. They find expression in dirges and curses, dark utterances, and a Celtic gloom in which everything is perceived as bad or a cause for despair. They are definitely not a people of indifferent mediocrity, but of passionate conviction, and that passion manifests itself in both uplifting and sometimes destructive ways."

"Why is that?" I wondered aloud, suddenly aware that I have been seized by such states at certain times (as JoAnne has reminded me). Without pausing, Sr. Columba said, "Oh, I think, it has something to do with their poetic and creative nature, as well as their latent mysticism that longs for perfection and union with God."

In the course of our conversation, after bringing in the tea, Columba unexpectedly brought up the topic of the Holy Spirit. Of course, I'd heard of this person of the Holy Trinity before, but she put it in the context of her own life. She said that she identifies so much with her namesake, Columba (or, as the Irish call him, Columcille), because of that saint's dedication to the Holy Spirit in his life. She asked if I knew of St. Seraphim, an Orthodox saint of eighteenth-century Russia, who had the same devotion. When I said that I hadn't, she suggested I read a booklet on him published by the Fairacres Press. I don't recall how we got started on the topic of the Holy Spirit, but I left the convent this afternoon with the lingering but persistent question about who the Holy Spirit really is for me; what sort of meaning this aspect of God has, if any? While I have been, as a teacher and theologian, much concerned with "the Spirit of Wisdom," I am more christological by nature and orientation; that is, I have been attracted more to the humanity of God, and have consistently addressed my prayers to Jesus as wisdom figure and spiritual guide rather than to the Holy Spirit. Now, as a result of the question Columba raised, I think I need to pay more attention to that other dimension of God, and perhaps make more room in my life and prayer for that third person of the Trinity. I see now, in retrospect, how adeptly and spontaneously Columba acted, even in such a brief meeting, as a spiritual guide.

Before leaving, we set up another time to meet. Then Columba raised one other topic with which I was in full agreement. Bringing out an old book on the songs and music from the Hebrides, those remote northern islands off the coast of Scotland, she handed it to me and said with conviction, "If you are going to study Celtic spirituality, you must learn not just from the history books, but from the music and songs of the Celts." I accepted the book and happily took it with me on loan. Her advice, of course, makes a great deal of sense, and I am looking forward to doing just that while I am here.

With Columba pushing me to study my topic of soul friendship from a more poetic and experiential perspective, while Benedicta challenges me on historical scholarship, I think I will greatly profit from both of these wise Anglican nuns' approaches.

Besides the progress on my research that I am beginning to experience in Oxford, there are the more mundane aspects of reality. I am totally disgusted with the mail system here. Postal workers have called a strike that could, they say, last months, just when I am relying on the mail for connecting with friends and relatives back home. I went to mail my letters this afternoon, and now the boxes are taped shut and the employees refuse even to take my letters. I can't believe the government allows international mail to be cut off, but Manus says it's Margaret Thatcher's plan: if the government does nothing about it, the public will soon be so irritated with the present postal system that they will come to accept the idea of a privately-owned mail system (which eventually, of course, only the rich will be able to afford). There was an item on the news last night how, after a year, the deregulation of bus transportation in England has created a rise in rates and less service to those living in out-of-the-way places. Great! But while I wait for England to get its act together, I feel caught in a mail strike that only adds to my sense of loneliness and isolation from family and friends.

Wednesday, September 7

Since JoAnne and I were in England three years ago, I have wanted to visit Newman's Oratory in Birmingham and his burial place at Rednal. When I was at Littlemore, I received helpful directions from Sr. Brigitte on who to contact and how to get there, so this past week I came to the decision to go there before getting too immersed in my research at the Bodleian. I made some phone calls yesterday, and this morning took a bus to High Street, walked the rest of the way to the train station, and then had a most enjoyable ride to Birmingham.

About 11:15, in bright morning sunlight, I arrived at the Oratory, the place to which Newman moved his fledgling community shortly after his ordination as a Roman Catholic priest. So many aspects of it reflect Newman's life and spirituality: the sunny courtyard with its hanging plants, the church with its very Roman Catholic (pre-Vatican II) interior, heavily covered with marble all around, and the pictures on various side altars of St. Therese of Lisieux, St. Patrick, and one of Newman's special spiritual mentors, St. Athanasius. (On a less inspiring note, I noticed reposing under another side-altar the rather grotesque "imitation" body of St. Philip Neri, clothed and fully visible to those who come to pray. I think it is a different kind of spirituality which believes that people today are fascinated or somehow inspired by skeletons covered with bits of flesh—especially imitation ones at that!) Overall, though, Newman's respect for the communion of saints, and his conviction that they really were intimate friends of his from which he learned much was evident in the art and architecture of the church.

One of the Oratorian novices acted as my guide, and took me to Newman's private rooms as well as to his library. I couldn't believe that I was actually there, seeing early drawings Newman had made as a child, the desk on which he had written his *Apologia pro Vita Sua*, the walls covered with pictures of his friends and students, and, most especially (for me), on his mantelpiece, the coat-of-arms with its three hearts, Cardinal's hat, and motto *Cor ad cor loquitur* ("Heart speaks to heart"). I noticed too a picture of another of his spiritual mentors, Francis de Sales, over Newman's private altar in his room, from whose writings Newman's motto had come.

After such a wonderful tour, I had coffee with the novice and then went back to the church for eucharist. There, I was surprised by the liturgy in which the celebrant still had his back toward the people, did not preach a homily, gave no kiss of peace, and had everyone kneel at the communion rail when receiving the consecrated host. It was as if Vatican II had not happened! Unlike Newman's ideas on development, the Oratory (or, at least, Oratorian liturgies) seems to have been unaffected by the liturgical changes of Vatican II, except for the vernacular. As much as I greatly appreciated the hospitality shown to me by the novice and Fr. Gregory Winterton who is in charge of the Oratory and who even invited me to eat a meal with the community, I still felt that I was in a mausoleum dedicated to keeping the memory of Newman alive, rather than in a vital faith community immersed in the latter part of the twentieth century.

I took a taxi to Rednal, the private estate where Newman and other Oratorians are buried, including Newman's special friend, Ambrose St. John, with whom he shares a gravesite. The taxi driver introduced himself as Ulrich Ewing, originally from Glasgow, Scotland, and he gave me a running commentary on every site imaginable as we drove. I thoroughly enjoyed his constant talk, and his assuring me when we arrived at Rednal that he'd wait for me until I returned. I opened the gate, and followed the path and sidewalk to the imposing stucco retreat center, shimmering in the afternoon sun. After exploring the premises in search of the graves, I finally discovered the Oratorian cemetery behind the building. I couldn't believe the quiet, peaceful atmosphere of the place with its row-upon-row of simple crosses. Since Newman's grave is marked like all the others, it took a little while to find. A clue, of course, in addition to his name, was the inscription on his memorial stone, *Ex umbris et imaginibus in veritatem* (from shadows and images into truth). I knelt and prayed at this spot of earth, made holy by the life of a truly extraordinary man whose vision far exceeded that of most of his generation, and whose life certainly portrays a painful and at times especially lonely pilgrimage from shadows into the bright light of truth.

I retraced my steps back to the patiently waiting Ulrich who asked me as I climbed into the taxi when my train was scheduled to return to Oxford. He then proceeded to give me (without charge!) a tour of the Birmingham University campus, to drive me by the Cadbury Chocolate factory headquarters (JoAnne's mouth would have watered), and to take me downtown to the Cathedral dedicated to St. Chad, one of the Celtic saints of Northumbria who had, with his brothers, been educated on Iona. That was an unexpected delight, to find myself at yet another Celtic shrine, especially one that I didn't know existed in Birmingham. All because of the gracious generosity of a stranger who acted as my guide. Ulrich's only response when I thanked him at the train station was to say, "Well, I wanted to do it; I hope someone would do that for me, if I ever get a chance to visit a foreign land."

The train ride back went quickly, as I talked the entire way with a young man from Liverpool whose parents were from Ireland and who was working near Oxford as a chef. When I arrived at St. Theosevia's, I cooked a supper of frozen fish and chips, and then studied for the rest of the evening. Savas stopped by my room about 10 P.M., and we went out for a pint of bitter at the nearby pub. He had finished reading the manuscript that I had written on spiritual mentoring before coming to Oxford, and so, over beer, we discussed its contents. He liked it, he said, and offered good suggestions for improving various chapters. He also suggested that I read the letters to "A" of Flannery O'Connor. I am not at all acquainted with them, since I have read so little of her works, but Savas seems to think there is something I could learn from them. I'll have to see if I can find a copy. I do believe that guidance in research, as in life, sometimes comes from the most unexpected places, and I am paying close attention to what I hear from those who live in Oxford.

I have really come to like and trust Savas, and am happy that our friendship is growing. All the house members are becoming companions here, accepting me into their lives with a friendliness and warmth that I greatly appreciate. Thank you, Lord, for another day full of fond memories and people whose generosity reveals your goodness and love.

Thursday, September 8

The weather this past week has been exceptionally hot. Yesterday in Birmingham felt like summer, and today has brought more of the same sunny heat. This morning I walked to the Medieval and Renaissance Centre. I am getting used to walking wherever I go, and, as my body adjusts to this new form of exercise, I am enjoying it much more, although at times I yearn for the convenience of my own car with the freedom to get in and immediately go whenever I want. At the center, I sat in on lectures by Benedicta on Early Monasticism and St. Augustine. She brings so much creativity and scholarship to her talks, blending together in a poetic and richly insightful way church history, literary references, and knowledge of Judeo-Christian spirituality. Following the lectures, I had lunch with Margaret Hebblethwaite at Brown's, a "yuppy" kind of restaurant down the street from Blackfriars and the Eagle and Child pub (where C. S. Lewis and his friends, the Inklings, used to congregate). She told me about her interest in the Ignatian approach to spiritual direction, and also what is happening regarding formation programs for the laity in Great Britain. Evidently, there are not all that many resources or programs available to lay people. She mentioned one program in Wales, and, of course, another at Heythrop College in London. Most of lay ministry is on a volunteer basis, she said, with few lay people actually holding paid positions in parishes or retreat houses. I found this somewhat surprising, since in the U.S. there are so many lay people involved in paid and volunteer ministries, while lay formation programs are available in thousands of parish and academic settings.

I spent the afternoon in my room studying the desert spiritual tradition, and for supper took a bus with Ciaran to a pub outside of Oxford called the Trout. It's a charming old place where, again, C. S. Lewis used to meet his friends, and is located right near a river with rushing, foaming water. What a great place to relax and enjoy not only the scenery outside, but the very typically British atmosphere within. We savored the wine and the house speciality, trout, and had a good conversation about Ciaran's ministry with the gypsies ("travelers") and his hopes for Toronto. Still, I missed JoAnne, and remembered how the two of us had tried to have dinner at the Trout three years ago, on our first visit to Oxford, but after a long (and expensive) taxi ride, we found to our consternation that the place was not serving food on Sunday evenings! Even when I told the proprietor that we'd come thousand of miles for a meal, he didn't seem all that impressed. (I'm sure he'd heard that line before!) So, we walked the grounds, sipped a beer, and then called the taxi back. By the time we finally sat down to eat at the Eastgate Hotel, back in Oxford, we had spent more money than we had wanted to—without eating a bite.

Saturday, September 10

I had a long dream this morning that I only vaguely recollect. I remember something about my parents having a new baby. If, as I've been told, the child is an almost universal symbol for the soul's transformation, I think the dream image must have something to do with the changes I've begun to sense in myself and my relationship with Mom and Dad....

All day yesterday I was in my room, writing a paper on the desert tradition of spiritual guidance, one of the chapters for my book that I'll show Benedicta next week. I finished at 8:30 P.M. and then went to the Lamb and Flag Pub with Ciaran and his friend, Patrick, who is leaving for the Ecumenical Institute of Studies in Dublin. It was crowded with young people, all "townies," which tells me something about what Oxford, at least its pubs, will be like when the students return in early October.

Today, from 9 in the morning until 5:15 in the afternoon (with only a half-hour lunch-break), I sat at the computer and typed my paper. It was very tiring, considering I had to learn how to use a new IBM instead of the Macintosh Apple that I am used to, as well as being constantly distracted by other people who are also using computers at the Computer Center. The good news, however, is that the center (one of the few in Oxford that rents computers) is only a few blocks from St. Theosevia's. I have almost finished writing on the desert, and will (happily) move onto the history of the Celts. Really, since first meeting with Benedicta, I have immersed myself in the desert studies, and certainly I will return to it. But after this weekend with so much immersion in the desert, I want to plunge into the ancient Celts and druids as soon as possible.

Lord, please keep my family and friends in your care. With the mail strike still going on, I feel very cut off from them. I was thinking on my way back tonight from the computer center, what a gift it is to know that we are loved. Although I am horribly lonesome, at least I know that some people even though far away love me. How do people survive who don't have any family or friends, those who have been deprived of them for whatever social, political, or personal reasons? It must feel like being half alive, and lead to all sorts of ways to fill that need to feel loved. I am now much more sympathetic toward the businessmen who are constantly on the road, away from home and family, trying to make a living. Sometimes the need for human touch and expressing affection is very strong in me, and I realize how lucky I've been to have loving parents, a wonderful wife, and two beautiful children of my own. God, bless all your children, especially those who feel unloved, and please have the bloody mail strike end soon!

Sunday, September 11

This morning I went with Peter to St. Giles, an Anglican church about a ten-minute walk from the St. Theosevia Centre, for the morning song and eucharist. St. Giles was first built in the twelfth century, and has a long and colorful history, including constant interior and liturgical changes due to the changing political intrigues following the Reformation. Restored in the nineteenth century under the influence of the Oxford Movement, it is a beautiful church with stained-glass windows, some marvelous stone figures and carved faces, and a men's and boys' choir that has a reputation (justified) for its quality. Although it was not all that filled for a Sunday service (evidently like many Anglican churches today), I was struck by its inclusion of lay people in the liturgical readings and announcements of the parish. Women, especially, were visible in the sanctuary, and at communion entire families were welcomed to the altar, including small children who received a blessing in place of the holy wafer. Peter took me over for coffee and cookies after the service, and I met a number of the parishioners, including the choir master.

I have now read the booklet on the Russian mystic, St. Seraphim, that Sr. Columba gave me. She is right about his spirituality reflecting a devotion to the Holy Spirit. Again, the question is raised for me: who is the Holy Spirit for me; what meaning does she have? I need to reflect more on this, but I am beginning to see the Holy Spirit wherever I go: from the Rublev icon of the Holy Trinity displayed so prominently in the front hallway of the St. Theosevia Centre (as well as over the altar in the Convent of the Incarnation at Fairacres) to Donald's mention of the Spirit in the Introduction of his new book, *Participation in God*, which I have begun to read. It is clear that the Eastern Orthodox spiritual tradition has a greater appreciation of the Spirit as a full, participating member of the Trinity than most of us in the Western church have.

Again, the quiet solitude of my room this afternoon has spoken to me of my past. I remember one dream in particular from about two years ago: I am with John, my son, in an ancient place with gardens and monastic ruins, and am told that the devil is coming. I am trying to protect John. An old man, not especially sinister, appears and points to me! I must come to him, he seems to be telling me, and he will reveal my sin. "You are a whited sepulchre," he says, "for you treat people without true compassion." Then he adds, "It is your sin and your form of suffering." As the devil, I remember, he didn't seem to be all that frightening, more like a wise old man. But what he said was!

Now I see that at the time of the dream I did "pride" myself on how compassionate and non-judgmental I was in my dealings with students and colleagues alike. That, of course, was the problem! Yet has any of that changed? In my solitude here constant memories have come to mind of my continuing lack of compassion: my deliberate hurting of John with my words on the trip, my outbursts against him, Daniel, and JoAnne when I was tired or so unhappy with my job. Even my last Sunday at home before coming to Oxford when I came down to the kitchen and saw that JoAnne had spilled the salad she had made for my going-away party all over the floor. What did I do? Instead of helping her clean it up, I returned upstairs, angry that any chances of intimacy between us had been postponed, and secretly thinking to myself about her accident, "What a stupid thing to do!" Then only hours later, after our friends had arrived, who was it that "stupidly" spilled the contents of the cardboard wine container all over the same floor? None other than myself....Was there a lesson for me in that synchronicity of accidents? Yes, I think so: my propensity to be judgmental, often of those I love the most.

It is the lack of compassion that often lies behind my temper tantrums when my anger is expressed as total unacceptability of the one with whom I am angry. I have done that with JoAnne too many times, with my children, my parents, and a respected colleague whom I hurt grievously with my rage. My friendship with the latter has not been the same, because of the hurt I caused. Aelred of Rievaulx is right. Anger that is poorly or self-righteously expressed can destroy the trust on which our relationships of friendship are based.

Lord, teach me gentleness, patience, and especially compassion, as well as how to express my anger more appropriately. The Desert Fathers and Mothers are right that "prayer is the seed of gentleness and the absence of anger." I think I need to pray more often; I think prayer itself must become a priority for me, not something I put off until my schedule clears up a little. With that excuse, I may never get started. I also need more leisure in my life, to take more time to relax and just enjoy myself and my family. I have been constantly pushing myself too much the past few years, and if, as a friend told me last January in Seattle, "leisure is the mother of gratitude," it's no wonder I have been feeling so burned out lately, and ungrateful.

Monday, September 12

I had another stimulating meeting with Benedicta this morning in which we continued our discussion on the history and spirituality of the desert fathers and mothers. I am gaining many insights into this spiritual tradition through my research and Benedicta's helpful comments. Before we closed our session today, she made reference to *The Golden Epistle* by William of St. Thierry and his recommendation that we have a picture or some reminder of our spiritual friends in our cell, so that they are always present to us, and so that we might remember them in prayer. An intriguing idea that I want to pursue. I will have to look for the book.

Following our meeting, I went to the weekly concert series at the University church, St. Mary's. The program of Phyllis Tate and Charles Ives's music was with violin, clarinet, and piano. Beautiful! And to think these musical offerings are available to anyone who happens in off the street!

Tuesday, September 13

I spent the entire day at the Bodleian reading about Nora

Chadwick's work on druids. I am becoming increasingly convinced as I do more research into the Celtic soul-friend tradition that the earliest soul friends were heavily influenced by the pagan Celtic shamans or druids, those spiritual guides who acted as "the living memory" of their people. According to the early legends, all three of Ireland's "holy Trinity" of saints (Patrick, Brigit, and Columcille) had druids as significant teachers and mentors when they were young. All three are also portrayed as spiritual leaders with the same powers often equated with druids, such as the ability to heal, extrasensory perception, and other psychic gifts that allowed them to see into the human heart and soul. Chadwick critically analyzes the various traditions about the druids, and quotes the classical writers, including one first century source, Pomponius Mela, who describes them as "teachers of wisdom, who profess to know the greatness and shape of the universe, and the motion of the heavens and of the stars and what is the will of the gods." Chadwick also makes reference to the presence of druidesses who in Ireland were called *bandruaid* and equated with seers, prophets, and poets who resemble, she says, "modern gypsy fortune-tellers."

Before beginning my research at the Bodleian, Savas and I had breakfast at Heroes, a tiny restaurant on Ship Street he introduced me to. It is always filled with people, and definitely has the most fantastic scrambled eggs at breakfast and curry chicken sandwiches at lunch. I heard a song there for the first time last week that caught my attention immediately. I liked the sound and the lyrics, and asked one of the students who the vocalist was. "She's American," the young woman told me. "Tracy Chapman's her name." I'd never heard of her before, but the album is played often over the sound system at Heroes, so I am getting to know her music which reminds me of the 1960s, and my earlier days of idealism and hope.

This evening, I walked to the Apollo theater on George Street for Andrew Lloyd Webber's musical, *Joseph and the Amazing Technicolor Dreamcoat*. It was the first of Webber's works, preceding his highly successful *Jesus Christ Superstar*, *Evita*, *Cats*, and *Phan-*

tom of the Opera, the one I want to see in London, but it appears they are sold out until well after I return to the States. I thoroughly enjoyed the enthusiasm and talent of tonight's cast, along with the choreography, bright costumes, and many references to dreams in the songs. Once again, I wanted to share the fun with someone, but, despite those lonely feelings, I found myself happily singing some of the lyrics walking back to St. Theosevia's.

I am feeling a renewed appreciation for the pleasure and healing power of music and songs, perhaps reflecting deep within me the beginnings of a rebirth of joy. My visits to Newman's Littlemore and Oratory seem to have made a great difference in my bouts with loneliness and my dark side, but perhaps what has affected me the most are the relationships of friendship, of heart speaking to heart, that I am finding here in Oxford. Nothing can take away the pain completely when we are separated from those we love, but friendship helps alleviate at least some of that pain, unexpectedly making it a little more tolerable and life more worth living.

❋ 3 ❋

To Cuthbert's Holy Isle
September 14–18, 1988

Now Cuthbert had great numbers of people coming to him not just from Lindisfarne but even from the remote parts of Britain, attracted by his reputation for miracles. They confessed their sins, confided in him about their temptations, and laid open to him the common troubles of humanity they were laboring under—all in hope of gaining consolation from so holy a man. They were not disappointed.

Bede, *Life of Cuthbert*

Wednesday, September 14
On the Train to Durham
Before leaving Oxford this morning, I went back to the Centre of Medieval and Renaissance Studies to hear Benedicta's lectures on Gregory the Great and his era, and on the Anglo-Saxons. The latter presentation included a discussion on Bede and Cuthbert. Her talks were a good and timely introduction to the journey I am now undertaking: to the city of Durham in northern England and

then to Lindisfarne. I decided that if I was to go to Cuthbert's "holy island" while at Oxford, now is the time, since Benedicta is leaving next week for Ireland to give a lecture there. I wrote Reverend Kate Tristram, a woman deacon who is director of Marygate, an ecumenical community on Holy Island which offers hospitality to pilgrims and scholars, and heard from an Alison Whitaker. She said that now was a good time to come, although Kate will be away while I am there.

So I am off on another pilgrim adventure, taking my books with me: Bede's *Ecclesiastical History of the English People* (which I am determined to finish one day!) and his *Life of St. Cuthbert,* a tattered copy that I've been teaching from and referring to since first reading it two years ago. Right now, though, as I sit here on the train and watch the autumn countryside rush by with its vast acres of green meadows and grazing sheep and cattle, something else haunts me.

I am coming to see that all my life I have been critical of my father, possibly because I feared him, especially his anger when it erupted, sometimes seemingly so suddenly; also I think because I felt that I never could live up to his expectations of me. What I accomplished never seemed good enough; what I couldn't accomplish seemed like the real standard by which he judged my excellence or lack thereof. He also seemed unpredictable, I mean his response to me. While others would always tell me what a wonderful man he was, so friendly, so understanding, (he was a tavern owner, after all), I saw or rather felt a different side: not only fear and panic when he became angry—his behavior seemed so unpredictable—but also great hurt when he told me as a child, "You're going to grow up to be a bum." Those words have haunted me for too long!

There's no doubt that he and I were different. When I was reaching manhood, we seemed to consistently be on opposite sides, including our political views, especially related to our involvement in Vietnam. When I was wearing long hair and wire-rim glasses, we almost came to blows one day over my appearance and "what the neighbors might think." At the time, it seemed to me, he was more concerned about how they might perceive him as an effective or ineffective father than about me, his "radical" son. Living in that small town with its own set of standards, he was obviously embarrassed by me, but, I see now the long hair was only a symbol of a much deeper estrangement.

In retrospect, I see something else: that I have never (seldom ever?) given him credit for being a good father. He was responsible, consistently putting in long hours at work, and putting up with, as he said, "the same old faces every day and every night." And he was also very concerned about personal integrity. I recall him at one point during my adolescence telling me that despite the tavern business, he had not developed a foul mouth and had always been faithful to Mom. His words meant little to me then, but now I am much more aware of how difficult it is to maintain personal integrity, and at what cost honesty demands of us at times. Dad put up with the day-to-day tasks and very considerable hardships of making a living, so that my brother and sister and I could be raised and educated well.

I love him, and I need to tell him that. I don't want to be critical or emotionally distant from him anymore. Time is precious now, as it always is, but I'm much more aware that our life together in this world, at least, is limited. I want to spend time with my parents and just love them without all those feelings and attitudes which in the past have gotten in the way.

Thursday, September 15

I am back on Lindisfarne, a holy place visited by a hundred thousand tourists and pilgrims each year. The cars and tourists have now gone, after another busy day. Coming here is having its effect on me. To drink deeply of the silence, inhale the quiet, lose myself in timelessness—that is soul-space. Cuthbert's Holy Isle, surrounded by water and accessible only when the tides go out, is a symbol of ourselves and our need for being apart from noise, busy schedules, and preoccupations which keep us out-of-sync, off-center, "beside ourselves."

Last night, as I came into Durham on the train in the dark with the lights of the city visible below the crest of the hills, I was filled with the delight of recognizing an old friend that I had first visited two years ago. Soon, however, my euphoria met up with the needs of every pilgrim to find shelter for the night. I was the sole person looking for a taxi, and barely caught the last one into town. The driver was not all that friendly, poor devil (I think he had just dropped someone off and wanted to go straight home), and then it looked like he wasn't going to get rid of me, since every place we went refused to take me because they were already filled. Finally, he took me to a bed-and-breakfast not far from Durham Cathedral where I got a small attic room.

By this time, I was famished, and went looking for supper, only to discover that most places had stopped serving meals. (The British seem to believe that everyone eats at certain designated times of day, and, if you miss those times, you're out of luck!) I ended up at an Indian restaurant, still open (thank God), and proceeded to sit there miserably in the midst of happy, laughing people, couples with their dates or spouses, all having a good time. By the time I reached my room and tried to get some sleep, my neighbor's television was on very loud and seemed destined to stay on for another hour or two. I was tired, unbelievably lonesome, and wondering why in God's name I'd undertaken to come here at all—not just to Durham, but to England itself! When I began to kiss the pictures of JoAnne, John, and Daniel that I had taken from my billfold, I knew I was experiencing more loneliness than I had ever felt before. There was nothing, however, that I could do, I realized, except crawl into bed, cover up my head, pray for help, and hope that this too would pass—including the television's noise and my neighbor's sleeplessness.

The next morning I took the train the rest of the way to Berwick-on-Tweed, the closest town one can get to if traveling to Lindisfarne by rail. When I arrived at the train station in Berwick and phoned Marygate House on Holy Island, I was told that due to mechanical difficulties with the community's only car, I would have to wait at the station until other means could be found for picking me up. So I waited—an hour, two hours, three and a half hours. It was a beautiful day, and I didn't mind the wait (at least for the first two hours) since I took my book on Cuthbert and moved outside and did some reading in the bright sunlight. I definitely felt better, despite the long wait, than I had the night before. "I am here," I told myself, "in the land of Cuthbert, my soul friend. Surely something good will come from this venture into the unknown." I had come, after all, because I felt that now I was ready to get to know Cuthbert better, and to enter into conversation with him in his home territory, on his own holy ground.

A man my age in a dirty shirt and khaki shorts finally drove up to the station, introduced himself as an archaeologist in residence at Marygate, threw my suitcase in the back of his jeep, and drove me across the causeway to Holy Island and Marygate where Alison welcomed me warmly. It is good to be here at last!

Alison, Nigel, Kajetan, and the others in Marygate community whom I've met are truly extraordinary. She took me immediately into the dining room for lunch, and introduced me to the staff, archaeology students, and my fellow-pilgrims who are also residing here for awhile. According to her, Marygate is an ecumenical community, now eighteen years old, which began originally as a sort of retreat center with occasional visitors, and has since expanded to two houses, one for guests such as the archaeology students and pilgrims who come and go, and another (called "Cambridge House") for people like me who want more quiet and solitude for longer periods of time. Full-time staff members make a commitment to community life for certain periods of time, depending upon their specific needs and some sort of discernment process with Kate Tristram. They work in the houses, offering their hospitality to guests, pray each morning and evening together, and often study together. Kate is warden of the community, but since she frequently travels, giving retreats and lectures and acting as a spiritual guide to women in the diocese, Alison as deputy warden is in charge. All of the members seem to be in their

twenties or early thirties, and here for a variety of reasons. Anglicans, Roman Catholics, Methodists, Baptists, and a Presbyterian,
they all share a love for Holy Island and its living heritage, the
Celtic saints. As Kate was quoted telling an interviewer on a show
by the BBC that I saw before coming over, "You really can talk
with them, you know!"

After lunch, Alison moved me into Cambridge House, and
then I was on my own. I toured the abbey ruins once again, what
remains of a Benedictine community that took the place of the
Celtic one founded by Aidan. These Benedictines were the ones
who had a special love for Cuthbert, as Bede explains in his book;
they were the ones who named Lindisfarne "Holy Island" as a result of the numerous invasions of the Vikings after Cuthbert's
death and the holy blood that was shed there. I went through the
new museum which had been completed since my last visit, and,
afterwards, on the grounds noticed once more the statue of Aidan
with his high forehead and Celtic tonsure, reminding me of my
own dream figure's unusual hair. "So," I asked myself, "what is
it, Cuthbert, that you have in store for me on this trip?"

Tonight, after dinner, I went for a walk by myself to the edge of
the island where the causeway disappears into the waters
brought by the incoming tide. It was a quiet moment, interrupted
only by the occasional splash of some fish off the shore, and by
the distant caws of the black crows in the trees.

I am looking forward to the morrow.

Friday, September 16

I share Cambridge House with two others: Michael, from Birmingham, a very talkative man about my age who has been a social
worker for years and came to the island for a week's rest; and
Peggy, a housewife and mother from Edinburgh, Scotland, who is
probably in her fifties, gray-haired, and a persistent smoker who
coughs a great deal. Despite the seemingly constant inclination to
talk or smoke, both of them are most enjoyable. We sat around the
peat fire last night, drank some Scotch, and told each other stories

about ourselves. At one point in our conversation, when I was telling them how much I missed my wife and sons, Peggy broke in and said, "But it's good for any relationship to be apart for awhile, and that's especially true for a husband and wife. I come here each year just for that reason, and, although my husband hates it, I can be much more present to him when I return. It's good for the both of us that I'm gone." And then she added, "Maybe it will be good for you too, and for your wife." The way she said it, so softly and yet with such quiet conviction, deeply touched me, and, despite my loneliness, her words resonated within.

I spent today pretty much by myself, reading about the history of the island, and more about Cuthbert. In the seventh century, the Christian convert, Oswald, became king of northern England, and sent for missionaries from Iona to evangelize (and civilize) his people. Aidan, the Irish monk from Iona, arrived in 635, began monastic cells for other Irish monks at Melrose (on the border between present-day Scotland and England), and then settled on Lindisfarne. Because of Lindisfarne's remote location and island-like qualities, it probably reminded Aidan of Iona, as Iona had reminded Columcille of Ireland. Lindisfarne and Northumbria were never the same again as a result of Aidan's ministries, which included training missionaries who went throughout Britain and eventually the European continent sowing the seeds of Celtic Christianity. This specific form of Christian spirituality had a great effect, I'm sure, on Cuthbert when he was at Melrose, and later as prior and then bishop of Lindisfarne.

In mid-afternoon I went to the parsonage where Reverend Dennis Bill, the Vicar of the Anglican church on Lindisfarne, had invited me for tea. We had a wonderful chat in his living room about the Celtic saints and his own life-journey that had brought him here. He was well read on the island's history, and, as I had picked up in the televised interview with Kate Tristram some time before, he too spoke of the saints as living companions and friends. He seemed especially convinced that St. Aidan had gotten short shrift from historians. "You know," he said as he leaned toward me from his easy chair and pointed his finger at me, "if it hadn't been for Aidan, Cuthbert never would have become the great person he was. Aidan was the one who brought with him that Celtic spirituality that was so formative for Cuthbert during his early years; it was Aidan who, years before Cuthbert used them, set aside as places of retreat that little island just off Lindisfarne and the Farne Islands where Cuthbert sought solitude and eventually died. Though they never met, Aidan definitely acted as Cuthbert's spiritual mentor, or, to use your term, as his soul friend. To understand Cuthbert, you have to know more about Aidan."

I appreciated our talk, as evidently did Reverend Dennis, since he invited me to stay much longer than we had originally planned. As I got up to leave for supper at Marygate, he walked out with me and shook my hand. Then I noticed as I left how he called one of the village dogs over, petted and stroked her affectionately, and seemed to talk to her in a language that the animal understood. Yes, I thought to myself, he too has been affected by the Celtic spirituality which pervades this island, manifest not only in lively conversation about the saints, but in a loving relationship with animals, a definite trait of those early Celtic saints, including Cuthbert and, of course, Aidan.

Saturday, September 17 (5:00 P.M.)

What a day of fulfillment, bordering on the mystical! So much has happened in such a brief amount of time that I want to somehow record it before I forget.

It began with my attempt (and Alison's indispensable help) to coordinate bus schedules, the schedules of the boats to the Farne Islands, car schedules of people at Marygate, and tide schedules (so I wouldn't be left stranded on the mainland in the afternoon). Despite this unbelievable amount of juggling, all went smoothly! I arrived at Seahouses, a small harbor town, by bus just in time for the 11 A.M. boat to the Farne Islands. Boarding with about twenty-five other passengers, I thoroughly loved being out on the waters with the spray of ocean water and the sun's bright rays. The weather made it seem more like a morning in summer than one in early fall.

As the boat took us toward the Outer Farnes which are an animal preserve, we saw hundreds of seals basking on the rocks and swimming near our boat, apparently unaffected thusfar by the disease which is killing so many of their brethren in other parts of the British Isles. We landed briefly on one of the Outer Farnes and toured a brightly painted red lighthouse, and then sailed on to Inner Farne, the tiny island where what Bede describes as Cuthbert's "yearnings of the heart" had brought him in his search for solitude. Setting foot on this ground made sacred by the presence of that holy man, I found it hard to believe that I'd finally reached the place.

As I glanced around, I saw only a few brick buildings, one of them a small church, another, something that looked like a tower, and, last but not least, a tiny building that I soon learned was the guesthouse built by Cuthbert's fellow monks to handle all the pilgrims who came in search of spiritual guidance from him. (The monks evidently did not want visitors to stay very long, since what is left of that guesthouse would make it appear that very few would have found a place to rest their weary bones, let alone stretch out to sleep!) "Well," I thought to myself, "here's one more pilgrim, Cuthbert. What are you going to teach me?" I crossed over to the church which was also quite small, ducked my head down, and went inside. There before me was a simple wooden altar with a few pews in front of it, and a stained-glass window above it, portraying in vibrant colors the figure of Cuthbert and some other saints. I knelt down and prayed, grateful to God for bringing me here. Then, since I had brought Bede's *Ecclesiastical History* with me, I read the passages from it describing Cuthbert's coming to the island and his final days on it before he died.

Since the others from the boat had only stopped for a quick glance in at the church, and then had wandered to other parts of the island, I caught up with them and joined them for awhile, enjoying the lush, green landscape and the cries of the seagulls. I felt called back, however, and returned by myself to the site of Cuthbert's solitude and ministry of spiritual guidance to be alone with the man.

Then something extraordinary happened that I still don't understand. As all of us were returning to the dock to board the boat once again, the tour boat was delayed for some reason. Rather than wait there where the group had gathered, I quite spontaneously decided to walk alone to the shore farthest away from everyone else. Alone on that edge of the shore, I found myself looking out over the water to Lindisfarne which was clearly visible in the distance. And then it came to me with a force that almost knocked me over. I remembered my dream of some seventeen years before: the first one I had ever consciously remembered that had come at a critical time when I was trying to decide what to do with my life. This was my dream, one that I vividly recall, for it was full of bright colors and loud sounds:

> I find myself on a shore, facing a vast expanse of ocean, and, as I watch, a thunderstorm approaches, the sky darkens, and flashes of lightning can be seen. The storm's fury intensifies, and in fear I turn away from the thunder, lightning, and churning water, and very methodically walk down the beach. There, in front of a brick building that looks like a monastery, I put on a religious habit, and enter the monastic confines that will, I hope, shelter me from the storm.

This dream had come when I was trying to make a decision on staying or not staying within the religious community to which I belonged at the time. Although I had never been told that dreams might have significance, especially at turning points in our lives, at the time I realized on one level that this dream was telling me something about at least one of my motivations for having joined the community in the first place. But I chose to ignore the dream's images, its message, and the guidance it might have provided, for

I really didn't know what to do with all that. Only later did I leave the community when I finally realized that, although I felt called to priesthood, I was not called to a life of celibacy.

Now, as I stood alone on Inner Farne's shore, I felt myself back in the dream! I can't adequately explain it in words, but there was a sensation that the dream lived in me, and I in the dream; somehow being on Inner Farne had reconstellated that part of me that I thought had been buried and forgotten. Realizing this (again, more intuitively than rationally), I deliberately turned on the shore where I stood, as I had done in the original dream, and faced in the direction of the ocean. Then I turned again—away from the water toward the buildings now standing where Cuthbert had once lived in his cell. I paused, and there on the sands and rocks I freely chose not to enter the monastery/cell, as I had in my dream, but instead decided to rejoin the group with the boat, to enter it and leave far behind the shore, the monastic buildings, and the island, and to sail back to my own life.

As I stood there staring, strangely feeling as if I had been here before, I very consciously re-enacted the dream in my imagination—only with the important difference at the end. This time I did go back to the boat and boarded it. Then, as we sailed by the remains of Cuthbert's island retreat, I felt in the depth of my being that something had now been completed; as if I were now more centered than I had ever been before, and somehow more in touch with my deeper self.

I'm looking for words to adequately describe some sort of inner soul experience, and I don't pretend to fully understand what happened to me today. It's as if my life journey had somehow been delayed when I had ignored the original dream's quite obvious message so many years ago, and had chosen to remain in the religious community to which I belonged. I don't know. I really don't see that time in my life as an "interruption" or my belonging to a community as some sort of mistake, for I am who I am today precisely because I was once a monk. But now it's as if I can get on with my life, without regretting the loss.

be that's it; maybe that's what today was all about: the need for me to live my life with less regret and guilt that I can't be a monk or a priest as the church presently defines those vocations, but instead accept that Cuthbert, the monk and priest, still lives in me, as my original dream about the Celtic figure with the high forehead and green robes revealed. He can continue to guide me, but rather than my attempting to totally identify with him, I need to be myself; to more fully embrace the loving community which is my family and more fully accept my own expression of ministry as worthwhile: this priesthood of the laity of which Vatican II spoke so profoundly. This trip today to Cuthbert's islands, especially to Inner Farne itself, is leading me to new awarenesses of my Self.

Another random thought. Although I am not Cuthbert the saint, his appearance in my dream has benefitted me personally and professionally in significant ways. I am becoming more the "Cuthbert" self imaged by my dream in January 1986; I am allowing aspects of him, of myself, to emerge. Without that dream figure, I may never have had the courage to move to full-time teaching and immersion in the further study of spirituality; without him, I may not have come to visit the various holy places and countries where the Celtic saints once lived. Because of him, I am able to more readily imagine myself back in those times as I walk the streets of Durham, explore the ruins of the abbey church on Lindisfarne, pray on Inner Farne where St. Cuthbert lived and died.

This creative use of my imagination, as well as actually visiting and living on this holy ground, is very necessary, I think, if I am to write about the Early Celtic churches and their important ministry of spiritual guidance. I think a person has to enter the past with one's whole self, body and soul, reason and imagination, if one is to recreate, as a teacher and a writer, the past for any contemporaries. I think one also has to be more fully aware with all of one's being how much the past truly is a living thing before one can help others discover that reality.

There is something more that I, again, am convinced words cannot adequately explain: the sometimes eerie sense that some of the people I am meeting in my journeying, such as Ciaran at St. Theosevia's, and Alison and Nigel and Kajetan here, I have met before, as if they and I were from much earlier times. Bizarre, since I don't, strictly speaking, believe in reincarnation!

My dreams and my deeper self, "Cuthbert," have led me here, and being away from my family, as painful as that is, seems to be changing me in an inner way. And I have only been gone three weeks! This time away, and the immersion in this time and culture, is a gift, and, as a result of it, I think I am meant to do something with it. I don't at this point know what that might be, but I am certainly not at all where I imagined I might be seventeen years ago when I had that first dream: on an island off the coast of northern England, encountering firsthand a man and saint who lived over 1300 years earlier.

I sense that I am now ready to talk with him as I sit at my desk in Cambridge House, and use my journal to pray. Turning to him as I write, I will, with the help of my imagination, open myself to what he has to tell me.

Ed: Cuthbert, I come to you for guidance as so many did when you lived here on Holy Island and on Inner Farne. I discovered today how much you are a soul friend, a part of my inner soul, and yet, a few years ago, I had never heard of you. I identify very much with you, not that I am a saint, for I know how unholy my actions have been and can be. No, I identify with your struggle to integrate your strong desire to be a good minister, intimately involved in many people's lives, with your intense longing and yearning for solitude. I identify with you too in your struggle to maintain unity with the larger body, the international church, while valuing your Celtic formation and spirituality. In many ways, as my research is revealing, although Anglo-Saxon, you were highly influenced by the Celts in your simplicity of life, love of solitude, connectedness with nature, and appreciation of spiritual friendship. Vicar Dennis Bill, in our conversation, said that he thought the best thing about you was your obedience to God and church: when you desired so much to be a solitary, you still agreed, albeit with great reluctance, to leave once more the quiet life you'd found on Inner Farne.

I realize now that though I am not you, in some ways my inner life and deeper self are reflected in you, your story, your life, and the dream this spring on your feast day could not be mere coincidence. You are a part of my soul and I continue to listen more closely to its quiet demands and invitations as a result of your presence in my life. It is true what Kate Tristram said that the saints are alive and can become very real friends of ours. We can talk with them, and they, in turn, will speak with us. Cuthbert, what do you want to say to me?

Cuthbert: You are like me, and I, across the ages of time, came into your life for a reason. I am the Celtic shaman in you whom you cannot continue to ignore: that part of your personality that needs solitude, prayer, communion with nature, communion with God—all those qualities associated with the early Celtic soul friends. Like me, you also seek to find a center for your life and to listen more closely to your heart; you also crave solitude at times and a cell where you can be alone—not by yourself, but with God. Seek God daily, despite the distractions and your responsibilities, and begin to value those near to you. Focus your love and attention on them; be kind and compassionate with them, as I was in the midst of my own yearnings for solitude. Be compassionate toward yourself. This is what I want to teach you: to be more accepting of yourself, your gifts and limitations, as you enter your second half of life. This is what your dream was about, the one of the Celtic shaman whose long, dyed hair you are afraid of showing. Why is it, do you think, that you are afraid of others seeing it?

Ed: I'm not sure, Cuthbert. It's a question that I have reflected upon often since that dream figure with his green robes
first appeared. I think he represents the repressed side of my
life, my spirituality, my Celtic roots that I need to accept and
integrate if I am ever to become who I am meant to be. But
what do you think; why am I afraid of showing my scarlet-
colored hair?

Cuthbert: You are afraid of the way people may identify
you. They might think you are not rational enough or too
prone to flights of fantasy. Most of all, you are afraid of
yourself and the change you might have to make if you acknowledge that side to yourself. You have spent so much of
your life attempting to please others in order to somehow
heal your own woundedness, to gain their acceptance and
love, to prove that, despite your father's words, you did not
grow up to be a bum. In many subtle ways, you have always
looked to someone outside yourself to tell you who you are,
and to take the pain away, the pain of living. But that is to
create false gods and look for false solutions to your pain.
Your life, your spirituality, *you* must be centered on God,
and no one else.

Ed: But I have tried to center my life on God. Years ago, I experienced God's powerful presence for the first time when I
walked in winter along the cold shores of a Minnesota lake
and cried out to God to accept my powerlessness, to take my
life into his hands. Later, in the love and forgiveness of a
friend, I felt healed and, as I had on the walk near the frozen
lake, a tremendous sense of liberation. Since then, I have daily tried to center my life in God.

Cuthbert: But you haven't always. You keep falling back
into old patterns that reassert themselves. You keep trying
to trust in your own powers alone instead of God's.

Ed: That's true; I am painfully aware of all that. But is that why you're here: to once more remind me of my inadequacies? God takes pleasure in his people, Psalm 149 says, and I am one of them.

Cuthbert: I know that, and I did not mean to give you the impression that that is not so. But you need me to remind you when you have lost your way, and become once again centered in your own illusions. I have come to remind you of a new level of centeredness, a new depth of integrity that is required of you in this, your second half of life. I am an image of your greater self: a monk, a hermit, a priest, a man of warmth and compassion who also knew through intense personal struggle how difficult it is to unite both the active and contemplative sides of life. I appeared to you in the dream to warn you and also lovingly call forth that side of you that you, in all your determined activities, were completely ignoring. I came to help you seek wisdom on a deeper level than you had imagined or were capable of imagining at the time.

Ed: But how, how can I change; how can I reorient my life in a direction that seems so unfamiliar to me, that seems more like falling into a void of darkness than a leap of faith toward God?

Cuthbert: Void or leap, they feel the same; they are one in the same. You must simply, despite your feelings, jump! God will catch you in his loving embrace. God has, in fact, already caught you, and the more you are willing in your solitude to look back over the destructive patterns of your life, the more you will be freed of them. One other thing: simplify your life. You cannot do everything, nor please everyone by trying to do everything. You cannot change the world by sheer determination. Simply be more present to the people you love and who love you; be more patient with those who irritate you with their demands, constantly distracting you, it seems, from your own schedule, routine, goals. Be attentive to them without looking to them to give you a self-worth and self-esteem that only God can give.

Ed: But where do I begin? How can I begin? You're asking the impossible.

Cuthbert: No, Ed, simply begin with prayer. You have already begun to pray daily since coming to Oxford. That practice has very much strengthened you, and made you more attentive to those and life around you. It is not as if the next life is when you need to be kind and compassionate; it is now. Both you and your wife have met profound personal limits this past year: JoAnne with an unknown illness; you with the realization how resistent institutions are to change. Learn from those limits to love each other *now*; learn to value those moments together with your sons and family *now*. Live in the present. Your soul is an "old soul," and while it values the living traditions of the past, your temptation is not to value the present, not to accept it, despite all its difficulties, with gratitude. If you learn nothing else from this trip, this pilgrimage, take gratitude and the discipline of daily prayer back with you. It is how I managed to deal creatively and well with my life and my responsibilities, and to die, with God's grace, in God's peace.

I have words of peace for you, Ed. I have words of forgiveness. I want you to know of God's love, manifest in so many ways on this pilgrimage. Be less condemning of yourself, and you will be less judgmental of others. Be less self-centered, even as the greater Self within you leads you onward. Learn also to say no when you so often would like to say yes. Discern your priorities, and attempt to act according to them as best you can. Take time to be away in prayer and solitude with God, so that you can be more present and compassionate to others when you are with them.

Underlying so much of this advice is letting go of your own mortality, for, really, much of your compulsive behavior is rooted in an unconscious race with death itself. As this pilgrimage has already shown, things will happen as they are meant to happen, so do not get so impatient and caught up in your own time-frame, and then in your impatience, take it out on your wife and children as you have in the past. "Let go, and let God" applies to you as much as it does to any alcoholic.

Ed: Thank you, Cuthbert, for your words, for your presence in my life, for your wisdom.

Cuthbert: One last thing, Ed. You asked about the meaning of the dream. The scarlet hair you saw in the dream was and is a reminder of how much Northumbrian spirituality is in you: that combination of Anglo-Saxon and Celtic roots. The green cloak, the emerald green cloak in the dream is a vivid reminder of your ancestral heritage from the Emerald Isle. You will learn more about that gift when you travel to Ireland later this fall. Whatever insights you receive on your pilgrimage travels, share them with others; teach others about God, prayer, and the communion of saints. It is conscious contact in prayer with this living communion that will change your life, as it already has in so many unexpected ways. Pray to Aidan and me, but also to those saints with whom your own life resonates: Aelred of Rievaulx, Julian of Norwich, John Henry Newman, Thomas Merton, C.S. Lewis, and your Grandma Mary too.

Ed: Thank you. Peace to you, Cuthbert, and to Grandma Mary, and to all the Anglo-Saxon and Celtic saints. May you all continue to teach me wisdom, but most of all, how to pray and to love.

Sunday, September 18
An emerging conviction of mine became more apparent last

night. That is why, perhaps, I feel a sense of inward turning. In a way, all that has gone on before in my life, all that preceded this trip to Cuthbert's Holy Island and Inner Farne, was a preparation. Now I am ready or, to be more accurate about my feelings, in the process of getting ready to return to my life, my country, my family, my occupation, and be as Cuthbert was: more genuinely accepting of myself, less guilt-ridden and driven (mad?) by my and others' expectations of me; perhaps even more grateful for both my gifts and limitations—out of which all ministry flows.

I have been reading the book, *Abba: Guides to Wholeness and Holiness East and West*, edited by John Sommerfeldt in which he writes: "Seeing or listening to the guru the disciple comes face to face with his true self in the depth of his being, an experience every person longs for even if unconsciously."

Reflecting upon Bede's *Life of Cuthbert*, I am beginning to see a theme emerging in his story. It is about a man who seems torn in two directions: between compassion and love that leads to genuine service and Christian ministry to others, and the unquenchable desire to be alone, in solitude with self and God. Cuthbert's life reveals this dichotomy, and it seems that it was never resolved in his lifetime. There were moments and days and perhaps weeks of being alone behind partitions on the Farne Islands where he retired in his forties with only a window in his cell for communication with the outside world. But always, it seems, he was pulled back into the human circle by forces and people beyond his control. Even in his isolation, people came to him across the waters, wanting him to act as a spiritual guide in whom they could reveal, Bede tells us, "the innermost secrets of their hearts."

But it couldn't have been just due to the yearnings of the people for good and wise spiritual guides. Surely it had something to do with Cuthbert himself. Within him there must have been a struggle, an ambivalence, for he always seemed pulled between wanting to withdraw into solitude (and doing so for awhile), but then moving back to be with people, possibly missing human contact because of his great love. How else can we make sense of his

great popularity, the attraction of so many to him, the genuine
love people felt for the man whom they affectionately called
"Cuddy"? People wouldn't have approached Cuthbert so insis-
tently and so consistently, if they didn't feel welcomed, accepted,
and loved from the depths of his soul.

Ah, now I am seeing more clearly how you, Cuthbert, dwell in
me. It is not only that your genetic heritage was primarily Anglo-
Saxon while your soul and spiritual heritage was primarily Irish.
Much more than that makes me identify with you. It is the polarities, the ambivalence, the struggle within that you represent. There
is something in me too that yearns for solitude, but also another
side which appreciates tremendously being involved intimately in
people's lives. That is the problem, and, I think, the possibilities.
My inner conflicts are the result of my strong eros, and I pray not
to be driven entirely mad by that spiritual side. Rather I pray that
I might learn to live more creatively in the tension that it causes.
Peace, my friend, and grant it to me please.

I got up this morning while everyone else was asleep, and went
to fetch the coal for the fire. As I went through the method of
starting it as Michael had taught me, I thought of Esther de
Waal's article on Celtic spirituality that I'd read in a recent edition
of the ecumenical journal, *Weavings*. She had written about how
the early Christian Celts, through their daily routines, including
that of lighting a fire at the hearth, found the presence of God and
the saints all around them. That was my experience, too, as I piled
the coals on top of the matted paper, struck the match, and
watched the tiny flame turn into a roaring blaze. Yes, the presence
of God and the saints....

I hate to leave the island; it has become a place for the soul, my
soul, to rest and be strengthened. It has also become a place of il-
lumination, quite literally, for after I had recorded in my journal
yesterday afternoon, something else happened to me.

I went to the prayer vigil in the church last night that had been
organized by the Marygate Community. I had eaten supper with
the community and helped with the dishes, then taken a long

walk alone along the beach near Cuthbert's tiny island, just off the coast, which was his retreat before he moved to Inner Farne. The night was almost pitch black with very few stars, so, as I walked and meditated upon the day's experience on the Farne Islands, I had to keep a steady watch on where I was going. I was praying quietly to Cuthbert when, just as I was turning to go back to the church for the prayer vigil, I happened to glance up to the heavens. As I did, I saw the white flash and slowly descending rays of a spectacular shooting star. "No, that can't be," I said to myself incredulously; "surely my imagination is running wild!" I put the wondrous sight out of my mind, truly thinking I had imagined it, until, as I stepped into the church, a woman from the community came up to me and said, "Did you see that? Did you see that amazing shooting star?!"

Holy One, who makes the wonders of this universe and who touches our lives in such profoundly simple, yet powerfully gracious ways, I give you thanks for your many gifts to me. Spirit of Wisdom, you have given me a strong sense of having completed something here, of integrating in me unknown aspects of my soul. You have also given me a sense of new beginnings. Be with me as my sacred journey continues to unfold.

❋ 4 ❋

Tokens of Love
September 19–October 4, 1988

The saints are not mere inanimate objects of contemplation. They become our friends, and they share our friendship and reciprocate it and give us unmistakeable tokens of their love for us by the graces that we receive through them.

Thomas Merton, *The Seven Storey Mountain*

Monday, September 19

I am back at Oxford after a long, crowded train ride from Birmingham in which I stood all the way. I spent last night in Durham, because I missed my connection to Oxford due to a slow (and another very crowded) train out of Berwick-on-Tweed. Faced with no other option, I went back to the bed-and-breakfast place I had stayed in before, and then walked around the city for the afternoon. It was a beautiful day visually, with bright sunshine accentuating the colors of the autumn leaves. I had brought my camera with me, so managed to take some very scenic views of families and lovers rowing on the river, as well as of the cathedral from the riverwalk with the old mill nearby. Then I once again visited the graves of Bede and Cuthbert in Durham Cathedral, and stayed for evening prayer. I had another lonely supper, and, to pass the time, took a long walk up the deserted streets and past the closed shops. Even in the rather bleak, drizzling rain, there is a beauty to Durham that I will always remember.

Today, I was relieved to finally be back in Oxford. Savas and I went out to the pub for a cold cider before supper, and then I spent the evening reading more about the Early Celtic Church.

I want to record one fragment from a dream that came to me last week on Lindisfarne which I had forgotten until now: I am home once again with my wife and sons, and am very happy.

Wednesday, September 21

It has been a month since I left home. Yesterday was a bad day. I think traveling can tire me out much more than I realize, and then going directly to the computer center yesterday with all its noise didn't help. I wanted to be home. I was tired of dealing with the English culture, and the many little ways we Americans live differently than the British. The one difference which I find particularly irritating has to do with the narrow streets and who is courteous or not. Tired and somewhat angry, I decided that I would no longer be the one who always moves off the sidewalk in the shopping area near St. Theosevia's so that others can pass by. I also looked for a heater for my room, since it has been getting so cold at night and there is no heat in the house "until October," Peter tells me. Then he added that adjusting to the weather and the lack of heat seems to always be "an American problem"—a comment, considering my present humor, I did not really appreciate! He was helpful, though, and suggested I borrow Donald's heater from the livingroom, since he is still gone. So I carried that up to my room and plugged it in. It was wonderful, and the heat that it gave off changed my whole attitude.

The heater is on now as I write, shaped as it is like a lit fireplace with the electricity pushing the tiny wheels behind the facade of the artificial hearth to make it seem as if there are coals burning brightly. I know it is not a real fire, but it has created a warm environment and pushed away some of the shadows of my room and of my life here.

Yesterday, for my praying, I purchased a small icon of the Holy Trinity by Rublev which I found in the shop at the University Chapel of St. Mary's. It is just like the one in our hallway here at the St. Theosevia Centre, and like the one above the altar at Fairacres. I am continuing to pray each morning and evening, sometimes with my hands outstretched briefly in the direction of my loved ones so many thousands of miles away, hoping that God's and my love will protect them from harm; praying that as they arise from sleep and begin their day God will support them.

Holy One, I am learning so much about England, and, by living here at St. Theosevia's, so much about the spiritual traditions of the East and West. Most of all, I am learning more about myself since coming here, and about what and whom I value. There are times, however, that I want so badly to be back in St. Paul with JoAnne, John, and Daniel. Savas, Manus, Peter, Ciaran have been a great help to me since I arrived, and so many others, such as the Hebblethwaites, Srs. Benedicta and Columba, have been kind and hospitable. I must not lose sight of that reality; I must not take my loneliness and homesickness out on others because they are different than me or because they happen to live in a different culture than the one to which I am accustomed. We humans seem inclined to be immediately suspicious of or to condemn what we don't understand, what is foreign to us, because, deep down, we want to find scapegoats for our unhappiness or for our fear of losing control.

The good news is that some mail is now finally getting through, and I heard from Mom and Dad, and other friends from the States. Also a card from my theology colleagues. It was good of them to write, and it sounds like they're off to another exciting (and tiring) year....I am grateful for their thoughtfulness, but for now I definitely do not miss the work. What I do miss is being in touch with JoAnne, being able to simply turn to her and share the happenings of the day. I will try to phone her, despite the great difference in time zones.

Thursday, September 22

I called JoAnne yesterday and spoke briefly with her and the boys. I appreciated hearing her voice at the other end, but she seemed very tense and began to cry, and said how difficult it was living as a single parent. Daniel evidently is taking all his anger out on her and John because I'm gone, and tells her that he wants to "go live with my Daddy in England." Somehow I knew when I left that he would be the one most negatively affected—from his immediate reaction when I first showed him the picture of Oxford last spring in the *New York Times*, and tried to explain my plans. He immediately responded with tears in his eyes, "Don't go!"

After hanging up, I felt very disturbed by the call. It seems that JoAnne is bearing so much of the burden of my decision to be gone, and, of course, my feelings of guilt have been reawakened. I don't believe that I don't care for them, or I wouldn't miss them as much as I have. The more I think about the call, however, the more I realize that for the sake of all concerned I need to return home earlier than I planned. From the advantage of hindsight, I now see how unrealistic I was to think that I could be gone so long without all of us being affected.

It feels right to return earlier. It is so expensive living here with the exchange rate what it is, and all I would be doing the final weeks of December is fighting with Oxford students for the use of a computer at the computer center, and probably in the weeks before Christmas cursing the cold weather as I tried to write in my room. Coming back home with JoAnne at Thanksgiving makes a lot of sense. I really think our plans for meeting in Italy for ten days before returning while my parents take care of the boys will also help the two of us get back on track with our relationship. I'll be ready by that time to return. My research and writing can continue at home, since I am now xeroxing important data at the Bodleian, as well as purchasing books at Blackwell's that I can read later.

Holy One, JoAnne is right that I have in many ways passed off to her the raising of our sons as I pursued my career and volunteer work for lay ministry. She's hurt and angry, and has a right to be. Please give her and the boys the strength to endure my being gone for two more months, and especially let Daniel calm down.

Friday, September 23

Another dream last night of horrible tornadoes sweeping in, but I survive.

At Benedicta's suggestion, I have started to read William of St. Thierry. A good spiritual writer, he uses creative images in his writing to illuminate theological insights, comparing love, for example, to the eye that sees God. "It is the kind of knowledge one has of a friend...that is direct and incommunicable; a knowledge of the heart that is too complex, too deep to be formulated in concepts or words, but that is nonetheless true." William advises that even solitaries should choose a person as a spiritual guide whose image may always be in their hearts, so that the more they recall that person in prayer and thought, the more they will grow like the person they seek to emulate. "The inevitable influence of a friend is to make one be like him [or her]."

Saturday, September 24

Kathleen (the sister of JoAnne's and my friend, Susan McLean) and her traveling companion, Ann, arrived in Oxford yesterday. I found them a bed-and-breakfast not far from St. Theosevia's, and then took them to dinner in the nearby pub. Tomorrow, we'll tour Oxford with myself as their guide. I especially appreciated a package Kathleen had brought me from home containing a Dukakis button, a white chocolate candy bar, and, most importantly, a letter from JoAnne and a tape with hers and the boys' voices on it, including the charming belches of my older son.

I was grateful to hear their voices and that of my brother-in-law Greg's, but at the tape's conclusion I was left with a horrible longing to see them again. Replaying the tape only intensified those feelings. JoAnne sounded better, however, and I was relieved to hear that Greg and Bobbie are back from Venezuela, since I know that they will be helping JoAnne with the boys. Thank God for the extended family! Now I know why other cultures value it so much.

Another pattern in my behavior has clarified itself for me that I will seek to break now that I am more aware of it. Besides the other two (i.e., expressing anger in such a way that it appears to be totally rejecting of a person's innate worth and goodness; and, disinterest in my children while they are growing up until they reach a certain age so that then we can communicate), there is my constantly complaining to JoAnne about my life. I remember Dad so often telling me what lousy hours he had, and how much he hated the work he was doing. Now I understand that he certainly was justified in his complaining, but I don't want that to be the only thing JoAnne ever hears from me. Being away, and seeing how so many other people live and the conditions under which they work has made me much more aware of reasons for being grateful.

Sunday, September 25

After Mass, I toured the streets and sites of Oxford with Kathleen and Ann on a cold, wet and windy day. Despite the rain, the beauty of Oxford in autumn is indescribable. The three of us walked the commons near Christ Church, peeked in at Oriel College, and stood in the street under the Bridge of Sighs and gazed through the fog to the Sheldonian. I couldn't believe how much I have now learned about the place, since arriving here in August. It has in some ways become a home away from home for me in a relatively short period of time. As the "official guide" on our tour, I engaged in a running commentary that included references to the city's history, names of the various colleges, as well as what other places were worth visiting. Evidently, I know more about this wonderful university town than I thought. I do continue to have ambivalent feelings toward Oxford, for it brings out in me not only so much love, but also moments of intense dislike, frequently associated with my dependency. I hate at times having to wait upon the bus system for my transportation instead of having my own car, and each morning I would give anything for a hot cup of coffee at some coffee shop near St. Theosevia's (there are none), instead of the instant stuff I now drink.

Much of this afternoon and evening I was in a movie theater watching *Little Dorrit*, based on a novel by Charles Dickens. A very delightful movie, but a long six hours—with only one intermission! Walking home in the dark, I glanced up at the brilliant full moon and couldn't believe how fast it seemed to be racing across the almost cloudless sky, and wondered if my loved ones so very far away would also see its shimmering beauty. I thought how we moderns so seldom look up to the stars or the moon any more, caught up, as we are, in what lies around us or the tasks to be done the next day. The ancients surely had a better appreciation of their lives, by taking time at least occasionally to look up and wonder at the mystery of the universe.

Monday, September 26

Donald Allchin returned from Denmark last night. I missed him greatly, and am happy that he is finally back. Quite honestly, in my admiration for the man, I felt let down that he was gone as long as he was, and resented his absence. Here was the mentor who I thought would teach me by his presence, and instead he had to be away teaching others somewhere else! Still, as a result of his being gone, I learned much by relying upon my own capabilities, and by taking initiatives on my own in learning and research. There is a paradox in that: how sometimes the absence of mentors can also teach us about ourselves.

An absent father. My father was absent much of my childhood, not at all because he was consciously neglectful, but his job made him very tired and just wanting to relax or collapse when he finally got home. As a bartender, he was with people always demanding his attention, and from my perspective now I don't know how he survived all those years. Nonetheless, he seemed absent to me emotionally and I deeply resented it without even knowing it, I think. Yet I didn't say a thing. I didn't know how to, or was I too afraid? Perhaps John and Daniel have those feelings....

I have been an "absent father" many times, an absent husband too, gone here and there for the sake of this or that commitment, too tied up, perhaps, with my idealism and myself, my ambition to succeed, to make a name, to be liked. As I have discovered this fall, I have not always shown an interest in my sons, in what they are doing. I don't want them, however, to grow up remembering me as being always absent, a nice guy "just responding" to other people's or different organizations' needs. The most haunting words I heard when I was a chemical dependency counselor were those from recovering fathers who were filled with regret that they had missed their children's growing up, and there was nothing they could now do to change the past.

I recall their anguish now, and I want to change: to reorder my priorities, to enter more intimately into the lives of my wife and sons, to not be "single-minded" about my work and ministry. What the desert guides called "purity of heart" needs to include first family and God, or God and family; and then my work. I know that when I return I will not be a perfect father or husband, but, Holy One, help me to be less painfully self-absorbed. The sayings of the Desert Fathers and Mothers remind me:

> It was said of a brother that his thoughts suggested to him, "Relax today and tomorrow repent." But he retorted, " No, I am going to repent today and may the will of God be done tomorrow."

My change of heart and new awareness must be followed by

daily acts of putting down my books and getting up from the computer.

Tuesday, September 27

I met yesterday with Benedicta and discussed with her Bede's *Ecclesiastical History* and the research that I've been doing on Cuthbert. Psychologist Rollo May writes, "The more deeply authors penetrate into the depths of human experience, the more they speak the language of all humanity." He goes on in his book, *My Quest for Beauty*, to define a "classic" as a writing or a person "that interprets our own deepest symbols or myths." I told Benedicta that Bede's *Life of Cuthbert* does just that, and that Cuthbert's life reflects our own inner polarities: the need to belong, and to give and receive love, and the need to become autonomous persons seeking to follow God's call to full personhood.

This afternoon I continued my research at the Bodleian, and in the evening had dinner with Peter and Margaret Hebblethwaite at their home. We had another lively discussion, this time focused on Paul VI whom Peter is writing about and whose papacy many of us are beginning to appreciate much more. The two of them also gave me some tips on good and inexpensive places to stay when JoAnne and I go to Rome. Since it was midweek, I left their house early, happy to have gotten to know these two people better, whose experience of church is broad and whose Christian faith runs deep.

Wednesday, September 28

I have found my place of study at the Bodleian: Duke Humphrey's Library. The oldest part of the Bodleian, it is filled with ancient manuscripts and stacks of venerable books, and has a beautiful paneled ceiling profusely decorated with the arms of the University and of Sir Thomas Bodley. On the walls are many portraits of medieval popes, kings, and statesmen. I have found a quiet place in the midst of this profusion of books and wisdom. I am making a great deal of progress in my research, inspired by the room, I think, and the stained-glass windows out of which I can look upon scenes of cream-colored parapets and falling autumn leaves. I am fascinated with the old documents on the Early Celtic churches, and the lives and legends of the early Celtic saints.

Thursday, September 29

I am sitting at my desk at the St. Theosevia Centre with the window open out onto the back garden and with the sunlight shining in. I have been listening to the numerous birds chirping in one tree as I read from a book on Irish poetry. The lines from the poem, "Scribe in the Woods" are especially enjoyable and, considering my environment, appropriate:

> A wall of forest looms above
>   and sweetly the blackbird sings.
> All the birds make melody
>   over me and my books and things.

Another of the earliest Irish monastic poems expresses well my experiences since arriving here:

> All alone in my little cell
> with no one for company,
> I love this place of pilgrimage
> now while I still have life.
>
> A hut remote and hidden
> for repenting of all sin,
> with upright conscience, unafraid
> in the face of holy Heaven....
>
> Christ, God's Son, to visit me,
> my Maker and my King,
> my spirit turning toward Him
> and the Kingdom where He dwells.

And let the place that shelters me
behind monastic walls
be a lovely cell, with pillars pure,
and I there all alone.

Great happiness fills my body and my soul. Yesterday, I made arrangements to return home with JoAnne from Italy in time for Thanksgiving. That seems very right, although I already feel some sadness in having to take leave of this beautiful place. My pilgrimage thus far has been one of synchronicity, and I know that I have gained a wealth of spiritual energy and knowledge. I am very grateful for what I have received, and feel especially peaceful about the decisions I have made. This afternoon I leave with Donald Allchin for Wales. I can't help but recall Thomas Merton's plans to visit Wales with Donald back in 1968, and how their plans for that trip were interrupted by Merton's unexpected death in Thailand. For years I have considered Merton an important spiritual mentor. He will definitely travel with Donald and me to Wales, and I hope to experience that country as he might have.

Friday, September 30

Wales' natural beauty has lived up to Donald's description of it, and, with its abundance of mountains, forests, and rivers, it definitely reflects what the Welsh call *hud*, that is, a sense of magic that the divine resides in everything around us. Since Donald and I arrived here yesterday there have been a wealth of memorable experiences. We reached the Skreen, a privately owned retreat house, in the early evening after driving through the Cotswolds and missing the Harvest Festival Service at a nearby Anglican parish by minutes, because of a late start and Donald's losing his way. He reads maps as well as I do, with the same sense of direction—or lack thereof—as I have. But he never lost his temper (an unbelievable man!) as I would have. He only said, "My, isn't this an interesting road to be on!" or exclaimed, "What a view!" when we became, as I thought, hopelessly lost, eventually driving down a road that narrowed to one small lane—only to meet at that point an oncoming tractor. But we got to our destination by hook and by crook, and waited in the wonderful kitchen of the Skreen for the owners to return from the church service that we'd missed. When they arrived, I was introduced to Antony and Mary Lewis, a couple in their thirties who were extremely friendly hosts. We got to know each other better over a delicious vegetarian dinner Mary had made earlier, one I enjoyed, even though not a vegetarian.

Today, Donald took me with him to Gregynog for a series of meetings which have as their purpose the planning of a national day in Wales honoring Ann Griffiths, a Welsh woman of the eighteenth century, about whom he has written extensively. He said that I could bring a book with me and read while he was in the meetings, but he wanted me to meet some Welsh scholars who might be able to help me with my Celtic research. "I also want you to see the national center called Gregynog," he told me. "It has a long history, many artistic works, beautiful gardens, and its own famous printing press." Again, I was not disappointed. After a quick two-hour ride across Wales in the car driven by Antony, we pulled up at a huge English tudor mansion that had been turned into a cultural center by the Davies Sisters in the 1920s, and is now owned, since their deaths, by the University of Wales.

While Donald and his group met briefly before lunch, I had a personal tour of the building and spacious grounds by an attractive red-haired woman from Northern Ireland, and then, following lunch, while the meetings resumed, I sat in the gardens reading my book and basking in the sun. It was a glorious autumn day (more like summer), and, as I read, the only sounds I heard were those coming from a flock of sheep grazing across the road from where I sat.

One of the high-points of the day was meeting Brendan O'Malley, a writer on Celtic spirituality who regularly organizes pilgrimages to the shrine of St. David on the coast of Wales. Donald had wanted to introduce him to me, and when he joined the three of us for the drive to Gregynog, he and I sat together in the backseat. We talked continuously for the entire trip. The more I listened to him, the more I had the impression of looking into a mirror. He too had been raised in a rural community and had joined a Roman Catholic religious community at an early age. (Unlike myself, when he discerned that celibacy was not his charism he became an Anglican priest.) He too was deeply immersed in uncovering Celtic traditions long since forgotten and presently under-valued by many contemporary Welsh. He too expressed the same tensions between communal/ministerial involvement (with a family like mine) and the strong yearning some days to be a solitary. Like myself who dreams of someday retiring to a cabin on a lake in Minnesota, he expressed the dream of retiring to a cottage on the shore of the Irish Sea. Both of us also described how we wanted to do more writing, praying, and contemplating on life's mysteries. (Of course, both of us will have to work that out with our wives.) Before the end of the trip, we issued reciprocal invitations that both of us and our families come and visit each other in Wales and Minnesota, and stay for awhile. I hope we can maintain this relationship of almost instant friendship that happened so unexpectedly. (It is eerie to meet someone who lives in another part of the world who appears to be so similar to oneself!)

Tonight we began the "Cloud of Unknowing" retreat for which I came. Based upon the fourteenth-century anonymous mystical writing by that name, the retreat weekend is being led by the Anglican bishop and spiritual writer, Stephen Verney. I had not heard of him before reading the brochure that Donald had left on my desk in Oxford back in August, but I was interested in pursuing the mystical tradition on "unknowing" for my teaching purposes, and, I think without telling myself until now, for personal reasons as well. Bishop Verney, with his white hair, friendly smile, and obvious compassion, is an excellent retreat leader, and he immediately moved us from an academic discussion of the book (which we were to read before beginning the weekend) to a personal one. Although I had planned to keep some distance between myself and the group by acting more as an observer and note-taker than participant, I soon found myself deeply affected by our discussion and by the openness of certain others in the group. A number of times during the evening I wanted to cry.

I feel as if I have been living the past year in a cloud of un-knowing, pulled this way and that from one crisis to another: from the great disappointment last fall with the Synod on the Lai-ty and the disagreements among ourselves at the synod leader-ship conference I helped organize in Rome to the strange illness of JoAnne that left her almost paralyzed before Christmas and on into the new year; from the information that there were those try-ing to have me removed from teaching because of my national work with lay ministers to the great anxiety whether I would ac-tually reach Oxford this fall when one after another of my plans fell through. I was left exhausted, and had come to doubt whether there was a God at all, or, if there was, whether such a seemingly sadistic deity could really be trusted.

Saturday, October 1

I realized something this morning as I brushed my teeth and glanced out of the window at the enveloping early morning fog: about my wanting JoAnne to say "I love you," and her telling me that although she doesn't always say the words, she shows me love everyday when she cooks, cares for the children, cares for me. It's true: actions speak much louder than words, and I've been unappreciative of the many ways she has expressed her love over the years.

Last night as I stood and gazed at the sunset over the Welsh hills and watched the clouds part and the sky light up with rose and yellow light, I felt my faith returning in much greater strength and at a deeper level than before: an emerging trust that God loves me and has all along though I have been too blind or angry to see. Yes, the synod conference did not go as I had hoped, but I learned much more about the dynamics of collaboration, and U.S. lay leaders will be meeting this fall to plan and organize themselves where we left off. Yes, JoAnne became ill, but she also got well when a series of tests helped the doctors diagnose the sickness and treat her. Yes, I had detractors at the time I was requesting tenure, but I had my defenders as well, and I did receive it afterall. Yes, I did not believe that I would be able to come to Oxford, but now I'm settled in that beautiful city, and meeting so many interesting people, including those this weekend in Wales.

Here at the Skreen I've gotten to know some of the retreat participants better than others, especially Nia, a lay woman who is active in promoting national justice and reconciliation in Wales, and Bill James, a former British soldier who is breaking my stereotype of soldiers. (He says that I am breaking his stereotype of the "ugly American.") All of us with our very diverse backgrounds seem to have come here in order to somehow deepen our relationship with God, many of us, I think, drawn by the theme of "unknowing."

I had a private talk with Mary Lewis this afternoon about how she and her husband, Antony, had become involved in retreat work. She mentioned the strong influence of Brother Roger and the ecumenical community he founded at Taize, France. They had visited there sometime ago, and been profoundly moved by the man's vision and his quiet search for a church that, while valuing the different spiritual and ecclesial traditions which have arisen in history, transcends the divisiveness of the past. Mary said that by opening their own home up to people for personal and group retreats, by creating an atmosphere of quiet meditation, and by inviting others to pray with them each morning and evening in the chapel they have built, she and her husband are trying to help others discover that same holy reality that the Taize community cherishes. She and Antony are obviously doing well from what I have observed. It is clear that having people walking through one's house, no matter how large, at all hours can be at times very inconvenient, not to mention cooking for such groups as ours, and cleaning up afterwards. But the two of them, along with another young couple, Paul and Carole Inman, seem to have a gift for making people feel welcome and comfortable.

I think what I appreciate most here are the times we pray together. The chapel is located in the loft of an old carriage house. It
is decorated very simply, with white walls and unvarnished
wood, and at one end is a window through which one can see
some of the Welsh countryside. Beneath the window is a small
wooden altar, and in front of that an icon on a stand. As at St.
Theosevia's and Fairacres, it is Rublev's icon of the Trinity. From
the start of our retreat, all of us were invited to join Mary and Antony for communal prayer which, like the interior of the chapel, is
very simply done: an opening song, psalms recited or sung together, a reading from Scripture, quiet meditation, and closing
prayers. Rather than using chairs or sitting in pews, we are given
prayer-stools which, because they are so comfortable, are condu-
cive to praying well. (They are highly appreciated by those of us
who are aging rapidly, and whose joints and backs ache much
more frequently than before.) Each prayer service begins with the
lighting of a candle in front of the icon, and ends with the smoth-
ering of the flame.

Sunday, October 2

I wrote JoAnne last night that being away from her has taught
me much about myself and our relationship. "At times I have mis-
used or taken your love for granted," I told her. "I want to start
again. Life is too short and unpredictable to take for granted anymore. I love you, and I will try to show it more explicitly from
now on. Please help me try."

It is a beautiful day this morning. Stephen Verney has been a
wonderful retreat leader, modeling how to be inclusive of everyone. Throughout the weekend he treated all of us with great respect, and attempted to include everyone's comments into our
discussions and his closing reflections. He personally set an atmosphere of openness that was contagious. Last night, he had
each of us spend some time sketching and coloring a picture of
some aspect of the weekend that has personally touched us. I
drew a rough picture (drawing is definitely not my talent) of the

Skreen at sunset, as I had experienced it my first night. Emanating from the dark clouds over the Welsh landscape are the bright rays of the sun, and emerging from the sun and clouds is the vague outline of a large, red heart. I have experienced much serenity and calm these past days; in many ways a rekindling of the heart. *The Cloud of Unknowing* that we have been reflecting upon this weekend seems to equate the reality of the heart with the work of the soul:

> Lift up your heart to God with humble love: and mean God himself, and not what you get out of him....It is the work of the soul that pleases God most. All saints and angels rejoice over it, and hasten to help it on with all their might. All the fiends, however, are furious at what you are doing, and try to defeat it in every conceivable way. Moreover, the whole of humankind is wonderfully helped by what you are doing, in ways you do not understand.

I am becoming increasingly convinced that those two realities are intertwined: to listen to the heart's stirring and to respond with love is, in fact, to discern intimations of the soul; and to be involved in soul-making not only changes oneself, but has some kind of benefit for all humanity—even though we may never know how or in what way. But surely that's a principle I learned from Alanon and A.A.: when we ourselves concentrate on getting healthier, our struggle has positive effects on other family members and the community-at-large.

The closing liturgy this morning had as its theme that of reconciliation. Bishop Verney presided, and at the conclusion of the liturgy of the word we were invited to offer our own petitions. My prayer was one of gratitude, as well as of seeking forgiveness from God for letting my anger and resentments get in the way of trusting him. In some ways, I am beginning to realize, I have responded to God as I have to my human father, and vice versa: resenting them for not responding as I thought they should; then sitting on those resentments and becoming, as a result, more distant from them; then blaming them for the feelings of alienation. How much better, as *The Cloud of Unknowing* advises, to drop the high expectations and demands upon them to act a certain way; to let God be God—and Dad be Dad. It's so much better that way, and in some ways so much easier. Playing God is draining and frustrating!

What I learned firsthand from the liturgy is that when I spoke about my resentments and anger towards God, I immediately felt released from them. It was as if I had to verbally acknowledge my sin before I could make room within for God's peace and serenity. Something else happened as a result of those people whom I had gotten to know this weekend. At various times following the service they individually came up to me and offered me words of encouragement and hope. Through their acceptance, I experienced God's forgiveness of me, no matter what I had felt toward him. Once again, I have been reminded of the importance of other human beings who mediate God's love.

Thank you, Holy One, for these people, for all that they have taught me, and for your loving presence in our lives.

Val, one of the women from the retreat, is taking me this afternoon to St. David's, home of the famous shrine of a Celtic Welsh saint, and a place I have wanted to visit for some time. Donald encouraged me to go, spend some time there, and return later by train. His advice has consistently been most worthwhile, so I am going.

One of the insights that came to me in prayer this weekend is how genuinely self-effacing Donald Allchin is. He does not just go through the motions of being polite, but is very sincere, friendly, and transparent with those whom he meets. I saw this at dinner with Antony and Mary the first evening we arrived: how genuinely interested he was in their activities, and how little he spoke of his own very considerable projects and achievements. And then, Friday evening, when the workshop participants arrived, he literally took a backseat, one of the seats farthest from the Bishop

Verney and one of the most uncomfortable, while the rest of us jumped for the most comfortable we could find. In his relationship with me before this weekend, he has gone out of his way to make me feel welcome, to suggest books I might use for my research, and to loan them to me from his personal library. He encourages creativity and scholarship; he is inclusive of others, and I have never heard him make any disparaging remarks. Now I see why he gets so many phone calls and why each day there is a stack of letters waiting for him, making the rest of us at St. Theosevia's intensely jealous.

Since he returned from Denmark, I am realizing how much he is teaching me by his presence, as his books on spirituality and ecumenism did before my coming to St. Theosevia's this fall. He is a significant spiritual mentor for me, and I am reminded of the desert fathers who allowed one or two people to come and live with them, and learn first-hand about prayer and the spiritual life. Donald, and certainly Benedicta and Helen Columba as well, are acting in the same capacity. I am humbled by their generosity to me, certainly a stranger to them until quite recently. The saying, "When the student is ready, the teacher comes," is true, as is Jung's belief that a friend or spiritual guide comes into our lives when we most need him or her. My own experiences in Oxford confirm this.

Donald has also put me in touch with the Welsh poetry of Waldo Williams and James Nicholas. I especially like two quotations from their works: the line, *Dy galon yw d'ogoniant* ("Your glory is your heart"), by Williams in his *Llwyd*, and the words from Nicholas's "Bardd":

The night of God around David's land,
Silent is the voice, heavy the flood.
Where is the heart, with its sea of light?
Where is the one great bard
    who gives us life?
Where is the hidden meaning of
    the master of song?

O youth, where is the passion?...
Old, very old is this gift—
This gift to unite men—
It is the heart, the well spring
Of all life, creating a better world.

Monday, October 3

I had no idea when I left the Skreen yesterday with Val that she would be taking me right into the precincts of St. David's Cathedral where she and her family actually live! Here I am now in the very shadows of the cathedral's main towers, in "the Cloisters" which is what their house is called. Her family wasn't here when we arrived, so she took me for a quick tour of the medieval Bishops' Palace located on the same grounds as the cathedral, and then we had dinner at a local pub.

Val, an attractive woman in her 30's or early 40's, told me that she is raising her children according to the philosophy of Rudolf Steiner, a man who believed, according to her, in the uniqueness of every child. "Each one," she said, "has a scientist, artist, priest inside of him or her that is waiting to be brought out. This can be done through a system of education that relies on artistic expression, ritual celebrations, and the use of the imagination." I was fascinated by what she related to me, and we got into a stimulating discussion on the differences in temperament children can have, despite having the same parents, and how each must be treated with equal respect. I thought of John and Daniel, and how often JoAnne and I compare the two. After our meal, Val dropped me off at the cathedral for an evening concert put on by a group of women vocalists from Israel. The music was beautiful, and, as I sat in the midst of this ancient church dedicated to David, the early Celtic bishop-missionary who is the patron saint of Wales, I felt once more that the history I was encountering here was a living thing, and that I would somehow be changed by my journey to the shrine and homeland of another Celtic saint.

Following the concert, I returned to "the Cloisters," and soon after Val's husband, Wyn, and their two children, Adam and Gregory, came home from a day of collecting mushrooms and other more exotic plants in some forest. The boys are about eight and ten years old, and I couldn't help but think of my own sons so far away. Living here with a veterinarian who is married to a woman who loves animals is, shall we say, an "interesting" experience. They have two dogs, numerous cats, and a new guinea pig in the house, as well as a donkey grazing in a nearby pasture which borders on the cathedral. (Five fox cubs, recently grown, are no longer living with them, I'm happy to say.) Whenever I sit down, I have to make sure I'm not sitting on one of the animals, and the largest, a Great Dane, literally takes up an entire couch!

I spent today touring the cathedral, a large stone and brick structure built in a valley, the story goes, so that the Vikings could not see it or its towers from the sea. (They still managed, however, to find it on a number of occasions, and raze it.) Inside the cathedral is a magnificent wooden ceiling with hand-carved coats-of-arms, a stone screen with statues of the saints, including one of St. David, and the tombs of himself and various other churchmen. I stumbled upon a eucharist being celebrated in one of the chapels near St. David's relics, and stayed to participate. Some of those who were in the chapel turned out to be Cathedral Canons gathered for a meeting that morning. A number of them introduced themselves to me after the liturgy, and then proceeded to introduce me to the Dean of the Cathedral who took me to the bookstore and pointed out which books on St. David would be most helpful for my research. I bought three, including a pilgrimage manual written by my old friend, Brendan O'Malley, and then went on to tour the town.

I stopped back at the house after lunch, and found Wyn at home. He asked me if I had been out along the coast, and, when I said that I hadn't, he graciously drove me a short distance outside of town and let me out near a retreat-house located on the cliffs overlooking the Irish Sea. The rest of the afternoon was unforgettable. I spent the time alone, walking along the cliffs for hours, mesmerized by the natural beauty of the ocean and of the land which bordered it. The color itself was breath-taking: a deep blue sea and gray sky that only accentuated the brilliance of the yellow flowers along my footpath and the orange and brown autumn heather on the hills. White crests of the sea came crashing up against the rocks, and sea and sky on the horizon became as one. It was a place and time when my soul breathed deeply and freely, and I felt as if I could reach out and touch the face of God.

I started out near St. Non's Chapel, a tiny building built of stone near the cliffs that houses the shrine of one of the great Welsh women saints, the mother of St. David. In her dark chapel with the sound of the waves far below, I lit candles for JoAnne, John, and Daniel, and asked that she protect them. Then, with the help of Brendan's guidebook, I pursued a solitary quest, exploring various ruins and holy wells along the way and was filled with awe at the spectacular view of the sea. Every once in awhile I noticed a plane high in the sky overhead wending its way toward Ireland, and at times I imagined that I could see the vague outlines of the Emerald Isle. Soon, I thought, I'll be on one of those planes, traveling to Maynooth to teach and write.

About midafternoon I encountered some hikers on one of the trails near the coast, and we walked together to a harbor filled with fishermen's boats. Although the hikers offered me a ride in their car which was parked nearby, I told them I wanted to walk on alone. Back in town, I went to a shop and ordered the delicacy I have come to appreciate at Oxford this fall: coffee, scone, jam, and clotted cream. (I justify this self-indulgence only by telling myself that since I am doing so much walking, the weight won't stay on. Ha!) After that wonderful "pick-me-up," I walked to Wyn's office and waited for his return, as did one after another townswoman, each holding a pet needing his attention and gentle touch. Soon, Wyn appeared, opened the office door, and ushered in his patients. As I sat there talking with each of the women, I felt as if I had stepped into one of James Harriot's books about his work as a veterinarian in England.

This evening, I had supper with the entire family. I really enjoy being with them and seeing all of them interact. Even some of the tension between Val and Wyn over domestic chores and who was to do them reminded me that JoAnne and I are not alone in that conflict. We discussed religion over the meal. Although both of them are very interested in spirituality, Wyn does not seem to want to have much to do with the church *per se*, and Val finds herself at times very angry with the lack of creativity shown by the institutional church, especially in a place so important as St. David's. "There's so much that could be done here for pilgrims like you," she said; "for one thing, we could set up a hospice and sponsor it for those who can't afford to stay at the places in town...." I told them about my wonderful walk along the cliffs that afternoon and my exhilarating experience communing with God in nature and solitude—with Ireland as a backdrop.

Tuesday, October 4

I am back at Oxford after a few days that seem, because of their fullness, to be at least an entire week! This morning Wyn drove me to a small village outside of St. David's where I got a ride with two women, Mini and Dorothy, who were driving to Swansea. There I bordered a train, and within a few hours was back at St. Theosevia's. Before leaving St. David's, however, Wyn took me back to the cathedral and showed me the tomb of Gerald of Wales which I had overlooked before. That was another surprise: discovering that this famous medieval pilgrim-writer-storyteller was buried right under my nose! His books on his travels to Wales and Ireland are considered primary sources on what those Celtic countries were like during the Middle Ages, and I, of course, have much affection for him now that I am visiting or have visited some of the same places that he describes so well.

I am looking forward to a very full week before leaving for Ireland.

Thank you, Holy One, for all that I learned in Wales, especially

❊ 5 ❊

Rag and Bone Shop of the Heart
October 5-23, 1988

Now that my ladder's gone
I must lie down where all
the ladders start
In the foul rag and bone shop
of the heart.
W.B. Yeats, "The Circus Animals' Desertion"

Wednesday, October 5

I spent today at the Bodleian researching the *Tripartite Life of St. Patrick*, after meeting with Benedicta and telling her about my trips to Holy Island and Wales, and what I had experienced there. She listened intently, and asked questions about Inner Farne and Durham. She also seemed genuinely happy that Donald had returned and had been so helpful in introducing me to the people of Wales. Her own presentation in Ireland, she said, had gone well, even though the weather was not agreeable.

I called JoAnne this morning and got her just as she had picked up the boys from day-care and was arriving home from work. It was *not* a good time to call! I was excited to tell her of my experiences and that this week I'll be going to the Sheldonian for a concert with friends from the States. But she was quite obviously tired and angry at me for being away. It turned out to be a disastrous phone call in which she accused me of always putting my career ahead of her and the boys. I was stunned by her vehemence, hurt, and then angry myself at her unfairness. She agreed that I could come, and now it's as if she doesn't want me to have positive experiences while I am here. What does she want me to do, put away all of my plans and goals I've had for years, and just return home?

Thursday, October 6

I got an early start at the Bodleian this morning, and had lunch with the Celtic scholar and historian, Richard Sharpe, who gave me some good suggestions for my research. This afternoon on my way home, I stopped at the Ashmolean Museum not far from Blackfriars. Savas had told me that a good collection of Pre-Raphaelite paintings was housed there, and I wanted to see them upclose. I was mesmerized by all of them, in particular those of Dante Gabriel Rossetti and William Holman Hunt. I had seen Hunt's famous "The Light of the World," depicting Christ as a Celtic-like king knocking on a wooden door, my first week here in Oxford when I visited Keble College. Today I was fascinated with his "A Converted British Family Sheltering a Christian Missionary from the Persecution of the Druids," as well as two others: one by Ford Madox Brown, "Chaucer at the Court of King Edward III," and the other by Frederick Sandys called "Gentle Spring." This work, strikingly beautiful, shows a woman dressed in white, standing in an English garden that has as its background a rainbow crossing a dark, forbidding sky.

Tonight was the party at St. Theosevia's that Donald had planned for Esther de Waal and Oliver Davies to celebrate the publication of their new books. I had appreciated reading Esther's writings on Celtic spirituality before; in fact, I had immediately felt that we were kindred spirits in some ways, so I was looking forward to meeting her. The party went well, and my friends Bill and Emilie Griffin from New Orleans arrived in Oxford just in time for it. Bill is promoting his book on C.S. Lewis and Emilie intends to do some research at the Bodleian while she's here. It was so good to be with them again, and I introduced them to Donald, Benedicta, and the others who had gathered at St. Theosevia's for the evening. Bill had heard of Benedicta before, and said that he wanted to talk with her. So he left for the kitchen where she was "hiding" for the evening, attempting to avoid the crowd. Emilie and I had a chance then to get caught up on our lives, and the time flew by. The two of them were tired from their travels, so retired early, while Esther and I, after the party had died, went to dinner at the local Italian restaurant on the next block. We hit it off right away, and took turns relating how we had first become interested in Celtic history and spirituality, and where it was leading us. She is a remarkable woman, and I am looking forward to the workshop tomorrow on Celtic spirituality when she will give a presentation.

Still, while all this has been happening, I have been preoccupied with my phone call to JoAnne, and I am not fully present to these happy events and people.

Since teaching John Bunyan's *Pilgrim's Progress* this past spring, I have identified with certain passages and stories from his book. The one that haunts me now as I feel so alienated from JoAnne is: "I saw in this condition I was a man who was pulling down his house upon the head of his wife and children; yet, thought I, I must do it, I must do it." According to a biography on Bunyan by Monica Furlong which I am now reading in my spare moments, "he [Bunyan] begins *Pilgrim's Progress* from the dilemma of every man who finds himself 'in the wilderness of this world': 'I dreamed, and behold I saw a Man clothed with Raggs, standing in a certain place, with his face from his own House, a

Book in his hand, and a great burden upon his Back..., and he brake out with a lamentable cry, saying, 'What shall I do?'"

I too am carrying a book, the one I hope to write; I too feel caught in the dilemma expressed in the question, "What shall I do?" I have invested so much of myself in this enterprise; I have so many hopes tied up in my research and writing, and yet it seems this creative endeavor which has met one obstacle after another has now encountered one more. Why doesn't JoAnne understand what this means to me? Why does she blame everything on my ambition?

Saturday, October 8

The Celtic Spirituality Day here at St. Theosevia's was well attended, and the three presenters, Donald, Esther, and Oliver Davies, did an excellent job. Oliver is a young author from Wales whose book on northern European mystical tradition, *God Within*, had just been published; he is obviously very talented. I thoroughly enjoyed the conference despite my tiredness. I have been sleeping poorly since my telephone call to JoAnne, and I know, as my anger, hurt, depression, and loneliness reassert themselves, my scapegoat is JoAnne. I could not believe how accusatory that last call was, and possibly underlying the accusations against me is her own fear, resentment, and feeling that her life is out of control. It is obvious that things are much worse than either of us imagined.

And my cry tonight, as it was yesterday, is that of Bunyan's, "what shall I do?" I can't leave now, break my commitments in Ireland, and lose all that I was to gain here and there, plus the financial loss of plane tickets to and from Ireland and Italy that cannot be returned. I feel that she has turned my dreams into ashes, bitter ashes, and I feel very cut off from her.

In many ways my dream of living at Oxford for awhile has proven to be most worthwhile, but very difficult to live with for the past six and a half weeks—for her and the boys, and for me. Yet I have learned, despite my extreme loneliness and guilt at being gone, that I do know already a great deal about Celtic history and spirituality as was demonstrated today at the conference. This inner affirmation of my own competence and of who I am becoming, experienced mysteriously at Lindisfarne and Inner Farne and with the falling star, may be what this pilgrimage has been about all along. I have been given more assurance of what I want to do with my second half of life: help resurrect, as my dream on St. Cuthbert's Day revealed, the Celtic spiritual tradition from the ruins of neglect and ignorance.

Despite my feelings of depression and anger with JoAnne, I met Bill and Emilie tonight outside the Sheldonian for the Vivaldi concert. "The Four Seasons," played by the European Community Chamber Orchestra's young artists, was unforgettable. I think I fell in love with the strikingly beautiful lead violinist, Adelina Oprean, whose brown hair, slim figure, and smiling dark eyes reminded me of the woman I married almost ten years ago. The entire evening with friends listening to music in that concert hall designed by Sir Christopher Wren was pure ecstasy, a religious experience that brought, for the moment, great joy, lifting me out of my depression.

Monday, October 10 (6:45 A.M.)

I am preparing to leave for Ireland today. Donald is giving me a ride to the bus station which will take me to Heathrow Airport, and then I will fly to Dublin in the early afternoon. Holy One, please be with me on this part of my pilgrimage; bless and keep my family safe; and help JoAnne and me to be reconciled. It is hard enough to reach an understanding of forgiveness when living in the same house, but trying to do so by letter or phone with so many miles between us seems impossible to accomplish. I want to, and yet I am still angry and hurt.

Yesterday was another unbelievable day. I met Emilie and Bill at their hotel, The Old Parsonage, and we went together to hear Donald preach at the University Church, St. Mary's, from the same pulpit as Lewis, Newman, Wesley, and others. He did very well, speaking eloquently on his favorite themes of remembrance, ecumenism, and hope, including, of course, references to the Welsh spiritual tradition that he believes is unappreciated by so many Britons. Then the three of us went on to Christ Church for Sunday eucharist. The singing of the choir was wonderful, but with the old-style vestments and the priests facing the altar with their backs to the congregation, I had the distinct impression that I was watching a pre-Vatican II liturgy, only with ordained men who also had families of their own.

Following the service, we took a cab to Churchill's grave outside of Blenheim, and while the Griffins went on ahead to the estate, I paid homage to the man who had helped save all of us from the Nazis. After praying inside the parish church, I walked to a pub, the White House, for a light lunch. The owner was especially friendly to Americans like myself, and the place had many photos of Roosevelt and Churchill, along with a large, colorful mural on the wall of Churchill and scenes from World War II. When I had finished lunch, I walked through a beautiful park to Blenheim, hiked out to the Victory monument and back in the falling rain, and then met the Griffins after their tour of the buildings that I had already seen on a previous visit. We drove back to Oxford, and while they went back to their room at the Parsonage, I began packing for Ireland.

In the early evening I took a bus to Oriel College and participated in its opening-of-the-school-year evensong. Again, I am amazed at the beautiful music of Oxford's choirs. There at the college where Newman had taught so many years ago, in the candle-lit chapel where he had once worshipped, I listened to young men and women dressed in red cassocks and white surplices singing with obvious conviction those old Wesleyan hymns with their numerous references to the heart. Afterwards, the preacher, a Scripture scholar, stood outside with his wife beside him, shaking hands. When I thanked him for a truly good homily and service, he asked me where I was from, and then graciously invited me to dinner when I returned from Ireland.

I took a bus back from Oriel College, and met the Griffins for a farewell dinner at the Italian restaurant where Esther de Waal and I had eaten. They will continue to stay here at Oxford for a short time before traveling to other parts of England.

All in all, it was a memorable week-end, and I am sad at leaving Oxford, knowing that I have so little time left here when I return from Ireland. It has more than met my expectations and high hopes, and all those experiences and relationships I will carry with me to my ancestors' native land.

I had a dream yesterday morning, the day of the Celtic Spirituality Conference. In it, I am telling my son, John, very tentatively: "I think perhaps I can now return to my teaching."

Tuesday, October 11

I am at Maynooth, located some sixteen miles outside of Dublin and home of the oldest Roman Catholic seminary in Ireland. Ronan Drury picked me up at the airport, and we stopped for coffee and apple pie with cream on the way to St. Patrick's College. I have two rooms overlooking the inner courtyard, with the church and its high tower all in view. There is also a wonderful fireplace to use every evening, with a pile of peat stacked nearby. I settled in, walked around town, and then after supper did some more exploring with Ronan. He invited me back to his room for a glass of Irish whiskey, and then I returned to my room to stare into the peat-fire and listen to music until midnight.

This morning as a visiting professor I had breakfast in the priests' dining room with Ronan and all the bishops of Ireland who are gathered here for meetings. Cardinal Tomas O'Fiaich, whom I met in Rome at the time of the Synod on the Laity, is also here. At noon the lay students of St. Patrick's College and approximately 350 seminarians (no apparent vocation shortage here) had the opening liturgy of the school year. In a number of ways, it was a very moving experience. I discovered that it is not only Anglican young people at Oriel College who can sing with such conviction, but young people here in Ireland at a Roman Catholic college as well. During the eucharist, I also had the very vivid impression that all my Irish ancestors were gathered there around the altar with us, the living, and that together we made up a communion transcending time and space. They seemed very real to me, very much alive, and I was made aware of the great glory—and suffering—throughout the history of the Irish Church. It is here where I feel so much at home.

I talked briefly with Cardinal O'Fiaich following his dedication of a special room set aside for Irish art at the college, and he invited me to visit him at his residence if I should get to Armagh on this trip. As he said to me, "I remember your interest in the Irish *anamchara* tradition, since you are the first American to ask me about it." I chatted over dinner with Padraig O'Fiannachta, author, poet, and professor here at Maynooth who had been so kind to me on my first visit to Maynooth in 1984. He seems to be happy and doing well. Following the meal, Ronan introduced me to the President of Maynooth, took me to *The Furrow* office, and now I am preparing to go to the John Paul II library to discover what they have that will help me with my research. I will be spending a lot of time there, in between my teaching a spirituality course to the seminarians.

Thank you, Holy One, for bringing me back to the land of my ancestors, and especially for the warm welcome, expressed through Ronan's friendship and hospitality, at Maynooth. I am reminded of Bede's description of how so many students and scholars came to Ireland to study during the Dark Ages, and how they were received so hospitably and with great generosity on the part of their Irish hosts. Despite the years that separate us from the time of Bede, it seems not all that much has changed.

Wednesday, October 12

I met the Irish spirituality scholar, Dermot O'Laoghaire, for lunch today in Dublin. As I did the last time I was in Ireland, I waited for him at the O'Connell statue on O'Connell Street, down from the famous Dublin Post Office, and, through the pouring rain, looked for a tall, white-haired Jesuit who has acted in so many ways as a mentor to me since 1984. We had a most enjoyable lunch at a nearby hotel restaurant, and got caught up on each other's research and writing. Then, as we continued our conversation, we walked past Trinity College to a bookstore with a large selection of scholarly works in early Celtic studies. Somewhere along the way, I lost a new umbrella that I had just purchased in Oxford for this trip, and the return to Maynooth didn't help my disposition any either. Going back to the college, I had to stand for one and a half hours in a packed bus that seemed to fill up immediately every time it stopped to discharge some passengers. Next time the train! Then I went to the dining room for the lay staff where I'll be eating my evening meals only to be turned away because there was a special dinner going on for the employees.

Just as I was going down the stairs (feeling unwanted, resentful, and very hungry—definitely a bad combination), a well-dressed man and woman called out to me and invited me back. They said that they were sorry about the inconvenience, but would get me set up in the seminarians' refectory for dinner. So I had a good meal with four young seminarians. One of them asked me how I was liking England and Ireland, and I said, "Very well, except for being homesick for my family." Of the four, the three seminarians who had just entered Maynooth this fall all nodded their heads in agreement, and said that they couldn't wait for their first break, two days at Halloween, so that they could go home. From the looks on their faces, I was reminded of my own painful experience of homesickness those first days in prep school.

Returning to my room, I was struck with the realization of how important human kindness and hospitality are in our lives, an awareness deepened this evening by the unknown man and woman who helped me find dinner, and the seminarians who showed interest in an older stranger from the States. Unless we have experienced the insecurity and loneliness of being a "stranger," I don't think we can fully appreciate the great gifts hospitality and human kindness are. To be far from one's home and family

and friends, and to be welcomed into the human circle is cause for
great gratitude. It makes a person aware of how important that
tradition of care is in our Judeo-Christian spiritual heritage.

Thursday, October 13

Players and painted stage took all my love
And not those things that they were emblems of....
Now that my ladder's gone
I must lie down where all the ladders start
In the foul rag and bone shop of the heart.

When I read those words by Yeats, the Irish poet, on the bus to
Sligo today, I almost wept in recognition of where my life over
the past three years has taken me, and how much I have been
driven not only by my ideals for the greater involvement of the
laity in the life of the church, but by my pursuit of recognition.
JoAnne was right: my ambition has driven me at great cost to her
and the boys. Instead of a search for holiness and a desire to be of
service, my ego has been in control. Being away from her and the
boys, living in my own wonderful/horrible form of solitude, I am
increasingly becoming aware that I need to let go of what has
driven me for so long. There is no question, any longer, that God
is in charge, not myself, and while that has led to a great deal of
ambivalence toward God, it has also clarified what I must do:
abandon my need to control; let go of my familiar ways of doing
things. In the letting go, a death of sorts occurs, a death of the ego
and a death of the familiar ego-centered order I have attempted to
impose on reality. Birth occurs too, an unexpected new birth of
myself, stronger than I ever imagined, more hopeful, and more
joyful. This past year and this autumn in particular have brought
me to the bone shop of the heart, a very uncomfortable place to
be, and yet a place of painful truth that has the possibility of un-
shackling many of the chains which have weighed me down.

I have also discovered something else this fall: some degree of forgiveness. This unexpected discovery is, I think, why another poem of Yeats, "A Dialogue of Self and Soul," also touched me deeply:

> I am content to follow to its source
> Every event in action or in thought;
> Measure the lot; forgive myself the lot.
> When such as I cast out remorse
> So great a sweetness flows into the breast.
> We must laugh and we must sing,
> We are blest by everything,
> Everything we look upon is blest.

Being able to begin to forgive myself has not come without outside help. Certain people have received my guilt and shame, and led me to a new acceptance that I didn't have before. Mary Talcott listened to me over lunch before I left for Oxford as I expressed my guilt over the incident with John and Dad in the car coming back from the Black Hills. She acted as a soul friend would, and, in her compassionate listening, I began in some ways to feel forgiven. Then, at the Skreen, the entire group listened quietly as I confessed to them the difficulties of the past year and my anger with God at being so far away. And they forgave me, not only in words expressed by the widow who came up to me later and said, "I pray that things will be all right for you when you get back," but in the circle dancing we did out on the lawn at the end of the retreat—a sign for many of us, I think, of healing, of hope, of new life that is possible when we turn our hearts toward God.

But the mystery of my experience of new hope which came out of my being forgiven seems based, first of all, upon my acknowledging the sin, the fault, the human blindness; acknowledging it to others, yes, but first of all to myself. Thomas Merton is right. The acknowledgment of sin is our liberation and the beginning of our wisdom: a wisdom not achieved by our own efforts, so much as given by a loving, all-forgiving, and understanding God.

Friday, October 14

Now that the Irish bishops have left Maynooth, Ronan helped me move to the retreat house in the Japanese-style garden. It has three rooms: a study with a fireplace, a bedroom, and, best of all, my own private bathroom. I am all moved in, and writing now at my desk with a fire roaring close by, with my books (in increasing numbers) on the long mantle above the hearth. Along with the books are the picture of John and Daniel, the small icons I brought with me from Oxford, and the handcarved statues of Patrick and Brigit I purchased yesterday in Sligo.

I was on that bus seven hours yesterday, a trip I hope never to repeat! I got on the bus outside of the college around 8 A.M. and three and a half hours later landed in Sligo. I had wanted to come to Yeats Country and do some touring before beginning my teaching next week. And then, after consulting the bus driver, I was told that I had only about three hours in Sligo itself, if I was to catch a bus back today to Maynooth. That did not help my disposition, but I decided quickly to make the most of the time I did have. After walking as rapidly as I could to the Tourist Information Center, I was again given the unhappy information that I would need a taxi if I was to get out to Drumcliffe church in the shadows of Ben Bulbin Mountain where Yeats is buried, and other sites associated with him. Pressed for cash and having little time for an extended tour, I decided to stay in town and see what I could see. Because it was closest, I went first to the church where Yeats's parents had been wed and where Yeats had been baptized, then on to Wine Street and the shop of the famous butcher-turned-woodcarver, Michael Quirke.

Mary Ann Savard had enthusiastically told me all about him last summer in Chicago, so I introduced myself and also met his wife, Eithne. I ended up spending most of my time with them. It was as if we had known each other for years. Michael showed me all of his statues and spoke about the Celtic mythological figures, pagan and Christian, which he carved in wood. Eithne had her turn as well, telling me of her husband's Celtic obsessions, and how one day, when she wondered aloud how she would get their sons to school, he had slammed down the book he was reading and turned to her. "Ah, at last, I have gotten his attention," she thought to herself, "and he will help me with this task." Instead, according to her, he turned and said excitedly, "Can you believe it? I just discovered that there were men in early Ireland who were over ten feet tall!"

Obviously, a "long-suffering wife," as she described herself, she also related that "he never cuts the grass in our yard; he doesn't pay attention to the children; he's always off in a world of his own!" She said this humorously, but I picked up a touch of hurt feelings and some resentment behind her words. At the same time, she seemed proud of him, even somewhat fascinated with his obsessions, and obviously hopeful that he would be able to make it financially now that, as he told me, "I hope to have carved my last porkchop."

In addition to the stories of their personal lives which, of course, sounded vaguely familiar (I, however, cut the grass), I was in awe of the statues, especially those of Brigit, Patrick, and Columcille. Each stands about a foot tall, is carved out of beechwood, sycamore, or oak, and portrayed with symbols representing aspects of the person's life and ministry. Columcille, a poet and writer, is seated holding a book, a prized possession which may have caused the war that was responsible for his exile on Iona; Patrick, looking like an early Celtic shaman or King Arthur's Merlin himself, holds a staff that has been plunged through the head of a dragon representing Celtic paganism; Brigit, surrounded by a sacred fire, cornucopia, and holy wells, has features less distinct. She is carved as a mysterious figure who, viewed from one side, is intertwined with a goat (symbolizing paganism), and, viewed from another side, holds the face of Christ (symbolizing her Christianity). Since I could only carry two and my funds were limited, I purchased Patrick and Brigit at a very reasonable price, and asked Michael to carve me one of Columcille out of oak and send it on to the States, so that I would have the "holy trinity" of Irish saints.

When I finally got back to Maynooth last night, I lit the peat in the fireplace and the candle on the mantle, and began to pray to those saints whose images I had before me. The flames in that dark room brought out lines and features overlooked in the light of day, making it seem as if the figures were very much alive. I found them helpful for my prayer, putting me more in touch with those two saints whom the ancient *Book of Armagh* says were soul friends, even though historically it is highly doubtful that they ever met. "Between St. Patrick and St. Brigit themselves," it says, "there was so great a friendship of charity that they had but one heart and one mind. Through him and her, Christ performed many miracles."

I had a drink with Ronan, the theologian Enda McDonagh who was on my dissertation board at Notre Dame, and a priest from a nearby parish. Enda had invited us to his room, and he, of course, spent most of the time running in and out, talking with his secretary who was furiously typing a lecture he was to give the following day. This morning I went with Padraig O'Fiannachta to a reception in Dublin inaugurating his latest book, one on Celtic prayers. He introduced me to a very colorful Chesterton-like figure, Sean MacReamoinn, whose book on the 1987 Synod on the Laity I had just read, and we chatted awhile about our experiences in Rome. While waiting for Padraig, I walked across the street to St. Stephen's Green, and basked in the bright afternoon sunshine.

When we returned to Maynooth a little later, I went for a ride with Ronan and Nial, a young priest on the faculty, to a mansion that had at one time been the "Big House," occupied by a family who once owned all of Maynooth. Despite being halted by a loyal grounds-keeper after we had been on the grounds for awhile, it was a wonderful visit, especially back in the woods where Ronan showed us the "shell-house," a house almost completely covered inside and outside by shells of various shapes and colors, set beside a cascading river and a pond. "Legend has it," Ronan said, "that a woman once lived here who lost her lover in some sort of accident, and was driven mad."

Saturday, October 15

This morning I worked on the syllabus for the spirituality course I'll begin teaching next week. I also wrote a book review for *The Furrow*, on recently published spirituality books, including Benedicta's *The Desert of the Heart* and Donald Allchin's and Esther de Waal's *Threshold of Light*. This afternoon I walked about a mile to pick up my laundry. There are no laundromats in Maynooth—hard to believe considering that it's a college town. The only one around is at a shopping center a little ways out of town where you drop your clothes off and some women workers, looking very hot and tired, wash and press your clothes for a modest price. (I thought of Mom, when I saw the sweat running down their faces, and remembered her long hours of dry-cleaning, six days a week, when my brother, sister, and I were growing up.)

This evening Ronan took me to a reception at a former Guinness mansion, preceded by a quick visit to Newman's University chapel in Dublin. At the reception I met the former President of Ireland, a former ambassador from Great Britain, who told me he was a lay preacher in his church and a devotee of C.S. Lewis, and his wife, as well as other political and religious dignitaries. The occasion was Enda McDonagh's inauguration as President of the Irish Association, an organization of religious and political leaders dedicated to the encouragement of dialogue on many levels between the Irish Republic and Northern Ireland. Following the reception, all of us went to the Abbey Theater for a special showing of *Carthaginians*, a modern play by Frank McGuinness, an English professor at St. Patrick's College. This one was a powerfully disturbing tragedy with a heavy dose of black humor, and it elicited a great deal of ambivalent feelings from me. I didn't know, at times, whether to laugh or cry because of the reality of suffering behind the actors' portrayals, and I heard negative reactions from some from Northern Ireland whom I talked with at the intermission. All who watched, however, were impressed with the obvious abilities of the actors, and I came away with the realization that the city of Derry where the plot unfolds is a symbol, really, of the contemporary "troubles" being played out in both the Republic and the North in which so many innocent people are dying. I left deeply affected by the play, and aware, once again, of the complexities of the situation which no Americans should presume that they fully understand.

Sunday, October 16

I ate with some of the lay staff and graduate students tonight after spending the day reading a book on Celtic history and writing a letter to JoAnne. I had gotten through to her by phone the second day I was here. She had apologized for her angry response to me the last time we'd talked, acknowledging her own tiredness and feeling overwhelmed at times, especially with Daniel. Now, she said, he is becoming easier to handle, and she's finding with the help of others some time for herself. I told her of my resolve to be more present as a father and husband, and of my new sense of priorities. We both seemed relieved at finally being able to bridge some of the emotional distance between us, not to mention the geographical! I am looking forward to our time together in Italy....

Monday, October 17

I was intrigued by one of the younger priest's remarks to me at supper last night. We were discussing the course I was to teach, and I was asking whether there was an appreciation among the Irish of their own Celtic spiritual heritage. He said that many of the young people in Ireland today are totally enthralled with the "glamorous" side of the U.S., and quite ignorant of their own rich religious history and cultural achievements. He added that he had no desire on his part to visit the U.S., since for him it epitomized the problems that beset the modern world: increased poverty among those already poor, social injustices, reliance upon military hardware for security, materialism, etc. I agreed with much of his assessment, but also told him that there were also Americans attempting to change those social ills. (The news I'm reading about the presidential campaign, however, has not been very encouraging thus far.)

I began my first class today with twenty-eight students: all seminarians, except for a priest (originally from Hungary) and an Irish nun. As I called the roll (Brennan, Carberry, Carroll, Crowley, Cummins, Donnelly, Dooley, Downes, Gates, Larkin, McCoy, Murphy, etc.), it was as if I was at a St. Patrick's Day parade or an Irish pub in the States, considering the distinctively Irish names I called. (It is hard to believe I am actually teaching in Ireland.) I am struck by the personal idealism and commitment of these seminarians who appear to be very ordinary young men, not overly socially withdrawn or especially conservative. They are definitely "Fighting Irish," however, since there was almost a wholesale rebellion when they saw my course syllabus. I had asked before drawing it up, what I could expect of students taking an elective course. The president of the college said, of course, that I should expect a great deal of them, and Ronan said that since they were taking other courses as well I should be more moderate in my expectations. I guess I was not moderate enough! But I had asked for their response, and I received it quite readily—to my initial chagrin.

So now we're down to one short reflective paper, and a major paper at the conclusion of the course, along with hand-outs that I brought with me that they will have to read. I am looking forward to learning from them, as I hope they learn something from me. It's hard to believe that, for them, Vatican II is a very distant, historical event. My God, most of them had just been born when it was meeting! I must be getting old....

A quote I came across at the library today from a book on the life of Columcille by A. O'Kelleher and G. Schoepperle: "It is the parting of soul and body for a man to leave his kindred and country and to go from them to strange, distant lands, in exile and perpetual pilgrimage." The words lept out at me, resonating so profoundly with my experience of continuing homesickness. Sometimes I can't even look at their pictures, the ones of JoAnne and John and Daniel; the reminders are too painful. Loneliness makes me long for human contact, not necessarily sexual, but

certainly that at times. I feel deeply the need to embrace and hold
and express my love physically. Now I understand the reported
promiscuity of many traveling sales or business people who are
on the road so much of each month.

Tuesday, October 18

I found this today as I was looking through a book in the library on genealogies:

Fay. Name not very common in Ireland. Fays came to Ireland
with Anglo-Norman invaders at end of the twelfth century and
settled in County Westmeath. Name of some is O'Fiaich from *fi-
ach*, a raven. Their descendants are now usually called Foy and
sometimes Fee.

Dear Martin Foy, my great, great grandfather,
Through Grandma Mary, I identify very much with you and
I want to speak with you tonight. I was reading today about
County Mayo where you once lived and about its history.
That history includes the abbot of Lindisfarne, Colman, who
returned to Ireland and settled in County Mayo after the
Synod of Whitby's rejection of certain forms of Irish spirituality in the seventh century. It includes Tirechan, the sev-
enth-century bishop who wrote a memoir of St. Patrick that
survives in the early ninth-century *Book of Armagh*, one of
the most important works on Patrick we have. It includes
the legends and sites in Mayo associated with St. Patrick
himself, such well-known ancient churches as Ballintuber
Abbey and such artistic works as the beautiful Cross of
Cong. County Mayo may even have been, according to one
source, the place where the people lived who appeared in
Patrick's dream calling him back to Ireland. Now I am more
aware how rich is the history of my ancestors', the Foys' history, your history, and appreciative that, because of you,
that history is mine as well.
I also read about the horrible famines and fevers of the

1840s which were quite probably part of your own memories. I respect you a great deal, for the trials you experienced growing up, and the hope and courage that drew you to another country. That must have been very difficult, remembering, as I'm sure you did, the land you had left behind, and, most of all, the many people you loved and who loved you. But if you had not had the courage to leave Ireland, my Grandma Mary would not have been born in Minnesota, and I probably would not have had an ancestor such as you.

Thank you for your courage and especially for your love. Thank you for taking the time to write down the story of your journey from Ireland to Canada and then to Minnesota. Grandma gave me a copy of it long ago, and it has helped me understand a little more clearly my own spiritual inheritance. I am sorry you and your loved ones suffered so much from the famine, the disease, and the poverty of your time. Please remember me and my family to a loving God, and to Grandma Mary and Grandpa John.

Tuesday, October 18

In Maynooth's library I came across an article by J. O'Sullivan, "Old Ireland and Her Monasticism," in which he states: "The remarkable circumstance is that after Patrick's enslavement, this boy full of loneliness...developed within himself a deep well of spirituality. Under such conditions his spiritual transformation began."

I understand much more, because of my experiences this fall, how this deepening of Patrick's spirituality could and did happen to him precisely as a result of his loneliness. Loneliness, like our other emotions, has a purpose. It can teach us about our very human need for other people and our unquenchable thirst for God. We are not, and cannot be, totally self-sufficient. Yet, at the same time, uniting our hearts with the Holy One, it seems that slowly and very painfully our loneliness is transformed into solitude; into an experience of greater serenity in being alone.

This evening at "tea" (really, "supper" for me) I found myself reaching out to the two black graduate students from Kenya and the priest from Hungary. All of us have been gone from the countries we call "home" about the same length of time, but I have a family to go back to fairly soon, and they will be here indefinitely: in a foreign country with a foreign language, and other difficulties to overcome. Bless them, Holy One, and be with them; help them continue to find spiritual resources and strength in their friendship with you.

Wednesday, October 19

I did not sleep well last night. While I am more at peace with being alone, I still find myself at times longing for JoAnne and the boys. At the same time, I am so angry with the polls regarding the U.S. presidential election. Tonight's newspaper confirms my own suspicions: all those polled in favor of Bush say it is because he won't raise their taxes! A totally selfish and myopic view when you consider the corruption of the Reagan administration, its flagrant disregard for the poor and homeless, its Central and Latin American policies.

Teaching seminarians is hard work. At times we seem to be on different "wavelengths." Some of it, I think, is cultural; some of it theological; some of it has to do with age differences. "Feminism," for example, is pretty much a dirty word here for many of them. It's associated with radical men-haters who want to tear down the church. When I referred to God as "he or she" at one point in my lecture, there were snickers from a few—and I hadn't meant it as a joke. And then regarding the Vatican II documents which I am having them read, I very much get the impression from some of them that the only thing Vatican II was concerned about was liturgical reform. Still, I like teaching them very much, and I especially appreciated Kieran Corcoran's questions arising from my lecture on the living presence of the past, the saints, and spirituality. "Are you equating the saints only with those great ones, like Patrick and Brigit, who are officially canonized?" he asked. "Aren't there the ordinary kind like ourselves who are, as St. Paul says, striving to live holy lives day after day?" I responded that I had not intended at all to give them the impression the saints were limited to only an elite; that, in fact, as Kieran pointed out, our ancestors, grandparents, parents, and all sorts of ordinary people can be considered saints from whom we can learn much about holiness and God. Kieran came up to me after class and introduced himself as a former seminarian who is completing his studies at Maynooth after deciding that his vocation did not include celibacy. He said that he hoped he hadn't seemed obnoxious, but that he always liked to ask questions. "You certainly don't need to apologize," I told him; "that's how we all learn."

I liked his forthrightness immediately, and, though I didn't tell him, he reminds me in some ways of myself, my own eagerness to learn. His desire to serve the church in a significant way, despite his lack of celibate calling, also resonated with my own life.

I had an interesting discussion tonight at supper with the graduate students. One of them mentioned how the Irish have a tendency to complain a great deal about everything, to see only the bad, and to expect the worst. That description sounds vaguely familiar. "Still, maybe it's not only an Irish characteristic," I thought to myself. "I remember Dad's constant complaints, and he's all German."

Friday, October 21

I awoke this morning to the rustling sounds of autumn leaves blowing against my bedroom window. Fall is definitely here. Even the beautiful trees with their many colored leaves in the garden nearby have now shed nearly all of them. At dinner today, the wind continued to jostle the windowframes and scatter the leaves outside. The season which I once dreaded, because of its close proximity to winter, is now one of my favorites, and the concert at the Sheldonian less than two weeks ago expressed so well the music and feelings I now associate with autumn. There are still roses in bloom here in Ireland, however, so it is quite mild compared to Minnesota at this time of year.

I had a very good experience yesterday in Dublin, despite seeing an old woman tossed up into the air by an oncoming car just as the Irish scholar Peter O'Dwyer and I were entering a pub for lunch. While Fr. O'Dwyer stood by the woman offering comfort and reassurance, I ran inside to tell the bartender to call an ambulance. Soon she was taken away, still conscious, but badly bruised, if not with broken bones. Quite a way to begin a lunch! I had not met Peter before, but we connected immediately, and he was most helpful and encouraging about the research I was doing on the Celtic soul friend. After I had asked about an early life on St. Brigit by Cogitosus, he took me to the Irish Academy and together we searched for and found a Latin translation I then had duplicated.

After Peter excused himself because of other commitments, I went on to Trinity College whose campus was alive with many students gathered in small groups talking and soaking up the bright afternoon sunshine. I climbed the steps to the Long Room, a library building dating back to the early 1700s that is lined with books and busts of famous men. It is also home of one of Ireland's greatest spiritual and artistic treasures, the *Book of Kells*. I had been to the Long Room on previous trips, but this time I noticed that the *Book of Kells* and the *Book of Durrow*, lying in glass booths, had been displayed in a new way, and that those two illuminated gospel books from early Ireland had been joined by one more.

As I stared down at the intricate designs of the three books, so intimately connected with all that was sacred to the Early Irish Church, I realized that something else was different than before. On this visit the *Book of Durrow* was opened to the illuminated page introducing the Gospel of St. Matthew. Now staring back up at me was "Cuthbert," my dream figure, my soul friend, the image of my deeper Self. Like seeing the falling star on Holy Island the night before I left Northumbria, I couldn't believe that it was he! Always before on previous visits the book had been turned to some other page. In amazement, I lingered awhile over this original piece of art, taking in the figure that I had only seen copies of

previously. Yes, there before me was the colorful robe, high forehead, and Celtic tonsure of someone who had become an important inner guide.

At the door, as I was leaving the Long Room, I glanced back at
the high wooden walls crowded with stacks of old manuscripts
and books. Suddenly I remembered the series of dreams that I
had had over the past two years in which I kept finding myself in
ancient, unfamiliar, oak-panelled rooms that are lined with books.
Again, like my experience on Cuthbert's Inner Farne, I felt as if I
was now back in the dream world. The dark wood pictured in my
dreams was there in front of me, and the strange room was the
Long Room with its treasures of Irish heritage—my heritage. It
was there that I had found the *Book of Durrow* with its figure introducing the Gospel of St. Matthew, a symbol of my own Irish-
Germanic genes that make up my inheritance of soul.

"So," I thought, standing and staring back increduously, "this
is what my autumn journey, my pilgrimage of the heart to Ireland
and the British Isles has brought me to." Despite all the difficulties and obstacles along the way, I have been led to my past, to
my soul's past, to all those ancestral components of my soul waiting to be claimed. Along the way, I've received help from many
unexpected places, and even the loneliness, the pain of separation, and my encounter with inner demons have contributed to
this sense of coming into my own, coming into my Self, coming
home. Sr. Columba said this time away might change me profoundly in unpredictable ways. Though I literally ache for my
children and my wife, it seems very right that I have come here;
though I couldn't adequately explain to JoAnne or to myself, really, before I left why I had to come, somehow I sensed that at this
stage of my life it was necessary to leave them.

Being away from them has helped me clarify what I want to do
now with my life: to be more fully present to them, my wife and
sons, my greatest gifts, and, second, to help others connect with
the spiritual heritage which is theirs. Those two loves, for family
and for vocation (what James Joyce so wisely describes as "the

call of life to the soul") will continue at times, I am sure, to be in conflict with each other. With the help of God, however, and my continued commitment to prayer, I hope that I can live with the tension more creatively and lovingly than I have before. Above all, I want my children to know that their father loves them very deeply, and I want JoAnne to know that our life together means more to me than anything else in my life.

✸ 6 ✸

COMMUNION ACROSS THE AGES
October 24-30, 1988

In the fellowship which the gift of God creates across the ages, we share with the saints a common history and a common life....In the communion of past with present which the Holy Spirit brings, the barriers of time are over-passed.
                    A.M. Allchin, *The World Is a Wedding*

Sunday, October 23

I am at the Emmaus Retreat House outside of Dublin for the annual Furrow Theology Course, a weekend sponsored the past few years by *The Furrow* for lay people from across Ireland to come and hear theologians discuss various issues related to contemporary society and church. This year's theme is on "Life, Death and Resurrection" and the presenters are Margaret Hebblethwaite, Enda McDonagh, Dermot Lane, Sean Freyne, and myself. I appreciated seeing Margaret again so soon after I had left Oxford. I also enjoyed meeting all the participants, especially Maureen Groarke, administrative secretary for the Irish Commission for the Laity, whom I had met in Rome at the time of the synod, and, for the first time, Ben Kimmerling, a woman with whom I had corresponded before the synod began.

Last night I gave my talk, "U.S. Catholic Laity After the Synod," and ended it on a personal note:

It is good to be back again in the land of my ancestors where my soul often feels most at home. I left the States in August, feeling tired after years of teaching and involvement with lay concerns; dejected too about the lack of progress women and lay people are making in the church. But I visited Newman's grave outside of Birmingham, England, and was reminded of his loyalty to the church of his day, despite so many years of feeling under suspicion by both Anglicans and Roman Catholics alike. I visited Wales and made a retreat in which I began to experience once again an emerging grateful heart. Last week, I went to Sligo and the land of Yeats, and in the poetry of that great Irish mystic, as well as in the warm welcome I received at Maynooth by ordained and lay people alike, I have experienced a rebirth of hope. Yeats's words, composed some sixty years ago, remind us all of the need to cast out any personal remorse or despair we might feel about the lack of progress in the church, for there are greater realities:

We must laugh and we must sing,
We are blest by everything,
Everything we look upon is blest.

The response to the talk was good, and I stayed up late talking with Ben and others who are also concerned about the future of the church. Some of them mentioned the increasing lack of local consultation in Ireland in the selection and appointment of bishops, and one couple stated how a new archbishop spends more time in his homilies quoting the pope than quoting Jesus himself.

Tonight, I met with the spiritual directors of Maynooth to discuss that form of ministry as it is developing in the States, especially the emergence of so many lay people, and women in particular, who are functioning in that capacity. The clergy and increased

numbers of women religious are evidently still the primary ministers in Ireland. Following our discussion, I went to Nial's room to
watch a late-night BBC show on the pope. The occasion of the television series was John Paul's tenth year in the papacy.

A somewhat superficial evaluation of those years was present-
ed, including a thoroughly misleading analysis of the Catholic
church in the States. What was most memorable for me, however,
was the way the show concluded: with a view of John Paul turning his face toward the camera. There he was, with the last frame
frozen in time, looking straight at the viewer: his eyes and the expression on his face revealing a vulnerability that is seldom
shown. It was a haunting picture of a leader who is perhaps not at
all that sure of himself; someone, like all of us, in need of compassion, the guidance of the Holy Spirit, and our prayers.

Monday, October 24

My teaching here is just about finished, and I'm preparing to
go to Northern Ireland for a quick tour before returning to Oxford. Since I have been reading so much about St. Patrick, I would
like to visit those sites especially associated with him. For some
time I've wanted to get to Armagh, and now that Cardinal
O'Fiaich invited me, I'd like to go. Still, I have some feelings of
trepidation, because of the political and religious turmoil in that
part of the country.

This morning I had a conversation with Betty, the woman who
cleans my room, about her daughter moving to the States in
search of employment. Outwardly so cheerful in our previous discussions, this time Betty seemed sad, and obviously very concerned about her daughter's future. "She just graduated," Betty
said, "and if she stays here in Ireland to teach, it may be another
three years before anything opens up in that profession." She is
evidently not alone, but one of many Irish parents today watching
their children not only leave home, but the country they call
home. According to various newspaper articles I've been reading,
during the past few years the Irish economy has slowed, and the

government has tried to control a growing national debt. Because of the job market, however, in which fewer job openings are available, emigration has increased dramatically, especially among the best educated of Ireland's youth. As a result of restrictions on granting visas to the States, many young Irish people are in America illegally. One of the pastoral issues facing the Irish bishops is how to provide adequate pastoral support to those young people, and most recently Cardinal Law of Boston has requested that the bishops send personnel to help.

I tried to assure Betty that since her daughter already knew a respected physician in the Boston area who offered her employment, she wouldn't have to worry so much. At the same time, I was reminded by the look of anguish on Betty's face and the anxious tone of her voice how often through the ages it seems to be Ireland's fate to see so many of her children leave families and friends for unknown lands across the sea.

I voted for Dukakis late this morning, after walking up the street into town to have a notary public officially witness the signing of my absentee ballot. That attempt to "turn the tide" was followed by a delicious meal at the home of Kim McCone, a young scholar at Maynooth, whose wife, like mine, also works outside the home. She was away, and he had cooked a meal of chicken with all the trimmings. His daughter, who is Daniel's age, was subject to the same behavior as Daniel: non-stop chattering all during the meal. I thoroughly enjoyed my time with them, and greatly appreciated Kim's help with my scholarship, not to mention the excellent food. I had to decline the wine, however, since I was teaching another class to the seminarians this afternoon. I spent the entire evening in the library, and now want to turn out the lights, stare at my peat fire, and pray.

Tuesday, October 25

I received a long letter from JoAnne today telling me how proud I would be of John's reading abilities, and that Daniel is "simmering down considerably, although he still has horrendous outbursts.

This morning he said, 'I want to pray for my daddy: Dear God, please take care of my daddy and keep him safe and don't let that sister blow smoke in his eyes.'" That sister, she said, refers to Kathleen whom I showed around Oxford with her friend Ann, and who smokes heavily. Evidently Daniel who hates cigarettes is concerned about my health.

JoAnne also described the presidential campaign as very depressing, and added: "I don't even feel like having another one of those sad election night parties we've had every four years. I will say it is a relief not to have to hear you rant and rave about the American people every morning during the Today Show, even if you're right."

I spent the whole day at the library, and had my last class with the seminarians. When I finished my lecture all the students stood and applauded. It seemed so spontaneous and somewhat raucous that I don't think it was merely being polite to "the American." A number of them have personally thanked me, and Laszlo, the only priest in the class, said the course was like being on a retreat. One student left a large candle in my room with a message that it might light my way "to return to Ireland someday soon." Teaching them was an education for me, and I am grateful it seemed worthwhile to them as well.

Coming back to my rooms through the Japanese garden tonight, I found myself stumbling in the darkness, since there was no moon to guide my steps. I remembered Savas' remark about his summer on Mount Athos, and how much the communities there rely on the moon and stars to get around at night. The moon is an important planet; perhaps that accounts for the great interest the ancients had in the path of the stars, the fullness and waning of the moon, and why even the Synod of Whitby in 664 was fought over how to properly calculate Easter, based on the moon's path across the skies.

Wednesday, October 26

I am writing this evening in my room at the Grammar School, next door to Cardinal O'Fiaich's residence and the Cathedral of

Armagh. I arrived in the land and city of St. Patrick late this afternoon. Fr. Liam, a professor at Maynooth, had kindly offered me a
ride. The journey was somewhat tense (for me at least) as we
crossed the border into Northern Ireland, not knowing whether or
not we would be stopped by the border police. We had to totally
bypass one town on the border because barricades had been put
up. With its police station surrounded by barbed wire, the main
street is vulnerable to bombings, Liam told me, and, in order to
avoid any catastrophe, all the roads leading directly into the town
square are periodically shut down. I had expected to see more police or British soldiers at the border, as they were several years
ago on my first visit to the North, but except for that town there
seemed to be nothing out of the ordinary.

We arrived in Armagh with a glorious red and gold sunset
lighting up the sky behind the twin towers of the cathedral, reminding me of my first evening in Glasgow, Scotland, over two
years ago. Liam took me straight to the Grammar School where I
was invited to stay the night, and, after settling in, I had dinner
with the priests and Christian Brothers who run the school, as
well as the Cardinal's personal secretary. Although the Cardinal
is away, he returns tomorrow and his secretary said he would try
to fit me into O'Fiaich's busy schedule. I am feeling very tired tonight. I was up early this morning anticipating all the moves, after
teaching the previous two days, in addition to doing research at
the library and at my desk. Still, I am happy to be here in Armagh. This morning I prayed for St. Patrick to be with me on this
leg of my journey, and he seems to be.

Tomorrow I hope to see the city and cathedral by the light of
day, and then go to Downpatrick and back to Maynooth on Friday. I have to go through Belfast to get to Downpatrick, and am
not anticipating being in that city of sectarian strife, but Father
John, a fellow alumnus of Notre Dame who is now teaching here
at the Grammar School, told me tonight over supper that it's
probably safer in Belfast than in Dublin. (I'm not so sure!)

I have met so many good people in Ireland, this home away

from home for me. In some ways I feel more rooted here than in Oxford, but I am sure that has something to do with my ancestry and my experience of soul. Meeting and being with people my own age, especially Ben Kimmerling, Gerry Mangan, Paul Murphy, and Pat and Mona McAuliffe, on the Emmaus weekend was particularly good for me. Ben told me that she knew Foys around Mayo where she is from, and invited me to visit her some day. Others in England and Wales have also spontaneously invited me to return and stay with them. Donald presupposes that I will come back. Right now, however, all I want to do is see JoAnne and the boys.

One of the things I want to discuss with the Cardinal, if I have a chance, is what I discovered in the library at Maynooth before I left: how the family name Foy seems to be a derivative of O'Fiaich. I must tell him when I see him tomorrow what Padraig O'Fiannachta said (in jest): that Foy was probably the illegitimate side of the family....

I have my "traveling roadshow" of icons (Jesus and the Trinity) with me, as well as my statues of Brigit and Patrick, and, of course, my print of "Cuthbert" from the *Book of Durrow*. I have been rereading my journal with Cuthbert's picture in front of me on the desk, and came across that series of vivid dreams about grand, ancient woodpaneled rooms with books and fireplaces. That has been my experience of Ireland. Besides the visit to the Long Room at Trinity College where I came upon the figure introducing the gospel of Matthew in the *Book of Durrow*, every night at Maynooth I have been following the same ritual. I build and light a fire in my fireplace, turn off the lights, and, while listening to Celtic music, sit and stare into the glowing flames. Slowly mesmerized by the dancing tongues of fire and the warmth, I fall asleep and then get up and drag myself to bed.

In some strange way, this immersion in Irish culture and religion has brought Grandma Mary closer to me. It's as if she is "haunting" me on my travels around Ireland. I seem to keep meeting her wherever I turn, and I even sense intimations of her presence in the rugged beauty of the land. I see her in the looks of stubborn determination on the faces of the old women on the crowded buses, in the people kneeling at prayer in the churches, in the happiness, playful humor, and give-and-take of families. Yes, I think I know her much better now, and love her all the more because through her presence in my life I have gotten to know and love the Irish people. I remember the dream that I had before I left for Oxford. In it my father, mother, Uncle Jim, and I are together when Grandma dies. I return to the room where she had been, and I feel her presence, a friendly presence, very much alive. It's as if I can see her physically, and I am not afraid of her ghost, for I know she loves me as I love her.

Grandma Mary still haunts my life, as the dream on St. Cuthbert's Day revealed when I found her in the ruins. She, like Cuthbert, is a soul friend to me, acting as a guide to whatever depths I have yet to explore in my search for integrity and wisdom. Sr. Donald Corcoran was right when she wrote me shortly after Grandma's death: "I must tell you that I had a very strong sense after talking to you that your grandmother is very close to you, will help you much, and that you should pray to her."

Dear Grandma Mary,
Thank you for being so much a part of my life. In many ways, Grandma, my spiritual and family roots—really, my soul's roots—have come through you, and I want to thank you for that and all that you have given me. You were one of my first mentors who taught me the "great realities": faith in God, love for one another in this life, and hope in the midst of dying. You always gave us, your grandchildren, a sense of being welcome and accepted for who we were, not for whether we lived up to your or our parents' expectations of us. You forgave us when we needed to be forgiven; you accepted us when we had difficulty in accepting ourselves.

You do stand, as I realized the summer after your death, in the Celtic tradition of women soul friends: strong and gentle, compassionate and challenging counselors, guides, reconcilers who teach wisdom not only through words, but, most of all, by example.

Mom told me about your death in the hospital; how you died, surrounded by your children, crying out your last words, "God bless my family, my wonderful family." When I got the phone call that you had died, in some inexplicable way, I felt orphaned: a feeling I thought could only come with the loss of one's parents. It was as if I had lost one of my closest friends, for you were always someone with whom I could speak openly and honestly in the language of the heart. I still feel at times an acute sense of loss. But time does heal, and it does teach us new awarenesses. I have come to see that our relationship did not end with your and Grandpa's deaths, but only changed to new and deeper levels of communication. I see now too that you made dying your life-work; that your entire life was in preparation for meeting God face-to-face.

Grandma, help me take steps, as small as they might be, toward greater wholeness and a less maddening way-of-life; help me to live a spirituality in which gratitude and joy are experienced more frequently as resources for my life and ministry. Help me to prepare for my own death by improving now the quality of my life, especially the quality of my care and of my compassion.

Thank you, Holy One, for this journey into my past, into my roots, into my soul. Bless Grandma Mary and Grandpa John and all my ancestors in the faith, known and unknown, who rest now from their labors.

Thursday, October 27, Ballynahinch, Northern Ireland
Well, I am here in a town that I had never heard of before, after

another tiring, yet fulfilling day. I had a quick breakfast at the Grammar School's upstairs kitchen this morning, and then toured St. Patrick's Cathedral. It is breathtakingly beautiful, with the full Celtic spiritual heritage set out before me in statues, stained-glass windows, and mosaics. I was thoroughly entranced by so much Celtic Christian hagiography and mythology in one place. With the help of a guidebook, I went from window to window, wall to wall, so as not to miss anything. And what caught my eyes especially were the windows portraying Patrick's dream that brought him back to Ireland as a missionary, the large and wonderful mosaic of Columcille with the island of Iona in the background, and the series of stories in mosaics of Brigit's life. One scene, in particular, was extraordinary: that portraying a bishop with his hands spread over Brigit's head. It seemed to confirm the early legends, and I am sure was a result of them, that Brigit, if not ordained officially, certainly had all the powers of a priest or bishop in the governance of her own monastery at Kildare. I lit five candles at a side altar for JoAnne, the boys, Mom and Dad, and Grandma Mary, and had to laugh at one of the women who was standing there when she said to me humorously, "Oh, a rich boy!"

I left the cathedral, and walked down the hill through the rather plain and rustic city center of Armagh, and on to the high ground, opposite the Roman Catholic cathedral, where the Anglican Church of Ireland houses its own cathedral. The latter is located on the original site associated with Patrick and his episcopal ministry. The church was deserted, and seemed cold and dark and uninhabited. It also appeared to be more British than Irish with its interior objects, plaques, and flags commemoriating various heroes and battles in the history of the British Empire. Relics of an original Early Irish Church high-cross in the back of the cathedral reminded me that, despite the Reformation some four hundred years ago (a relatively recent ecclesial development), the earliest history of the Christian church in Ireland, represented by the high-cross, bound all of us together, whether Roman Catholic or Anglican.

Still, a sadness overwhelmed me in this church that seemed so deserted by comparison with its Roman counterpart which across town on the other slope was preparing a huge eucharistic liturgy celebrating the union of three Catholic grammar schools. I knelt and prayed for church unity between those two cathedrals, symbols of two spiritual traditions and approaches to Christian life. I wondered aloud how the People of God could ever come together when so much "brick and mortar," power, prestige, personal identity, and tradition separate the two. Only Christ our bridge (to use the imagery of St. Catherine of Siena) and the creative power of the Spirit can bring about this unity for which so many yearn.

As I left the cathedral, I spied outside in the church wall a plaque pointing out the gravesite of Brian Boru, the only high king who had ever united all of Ireland, and then for only a very brief time before someone had assassinated him after the Battle of Clontarf in 1014. Then I walked down the hill and back to the mainstreet of Armagh. There, very unexpectedly, I was surprised to see policemen armed with rifles walking down the street while leading German shepherds on leashes. It seemed like such an ordinary day with mostly elderly shoppers on the streets and in the shops! The scene was a strong reminder of how closely violence lies beneath Northern Ireland's society, waiting to erupt. The people, however, have evidently grown accustomed to the sight of arms openly displayed, and didn't seem to even notice. They were warm and friendly to "the Yank"—as one old man called me, racing after me to ask if I knew some person in the States who was a friend of his. (I didn't.)

I climbed the hill to the Roman Catholic cathedral once again and joined the Mass in progress with Cardinal O'Fiaich presiding. He delivered a blustery homily, as only he can do, about the history of the Grammar School and how unity among schools (and within nations) has advantages for everyone. After the Mass, I caught up with him and joined him in the procession back to the sacristy. He was his usual warm and gracious self even though the day ahead of him was obviously going to be very busy. Back in the sacristy, he blessed the hand-carved statues of Brigit and Patrick I had brought with me from Maynooth, and then went back to his own residence to get a book for me on the history of the Roman Catholic cathedral of Armagh. Again, he apologized for not having more time to visit today, and invited me to stay for another night. I told him I couldn't do so, but that I very much appreciated the hospitality I had already received, and would keep him posted on my research. We continued to chat for awhile as the school officials lined up for pictures with him to commemorate the day, and, before leaving, I told him of O'Fiannachta's remark about the Foys. He laughed too, and said how he already knew that the O'Fiaichs and Foys were possibly related.

I really like the man. As a church leader, he is down-to-earth, intelligent, witty, and very supportive of the laity. In his own way, he reminds me of the personal, humorous Pope John XXIII who continues to inspire many people today both inside and outside the Roman Catholic church.

I got caught in the rain as I waited with about forty students who were also getting the bus to Belfast. Again, like downtown Armagh, there was the same sense of normalcy once we arrived in Belfast. In the midst of the violent "troubles" and much sectarian hatred, there were friendly people I encountered on the streets, all looking rather well dressed and unconcerned. I had to walk through the downtown area to another bus station some distance away to get a bus to Downpatrick, and was surprised how prosperous this part of the city seemed in contrast to the war-torn areas portrayed on television.

Once on this second bus since leaving Armagh, time seemed to stand still as I waited to reach Downpatrick. We finally arrived about five o'clock in the afternoon, just as the sun was beginning to set behind the beautiful Mountains of Mourne in the distance. A man at the bus station gave me directions to the parish house of Fr. Joseph McGuire, a priest whom one of my students at Maynooth had recommended that I see when I announced to the class that I was traveling to Armagh. A scholar himself in early Irish history, the priest was not in, but the housekeeper told me to come back around 7:00, and to leave my suitcase there. I went immediately in search of St. Patrick's grave, and found it in the lengthening shadows of an Anglican church. There it was: the huge, flat gray stone, more like a boulder, with the inscription "Patrick" in bold letters etched into the stone. It was too dark to take pictures, so I wandered back down the street and entered a Chinese restaurant for supper. After a wonderful meal, appreciated all the more because of the long afternoon and feelings of being a stranger in yet another foreign town, I went back to the rectory in the light autumn rain.

Father McGuire was waiting for me, and invited me in for an animated talk on Irish history and a view of an ancient painting of a blind Irish bard on the wall of his living room. I told him of my research, and eventually mentioned what Ronan had told me about St. Patrick's grave, that it was "all Irish blarney." Father McGuire smiled, having heard that remark before, and said with some conviction, "Well, it could be; we have no way of knowing. But I've always believed there must be some truth to all the tales linking Patrick with this part of the country. The stories go back so far, and so many common folk, in addition to some early historians, obviously believed them. I don't think we should overlook that bit of folk wisdom, and merely equate it with superstitious beliefs." Since he already had pastoral work to do that evening, he dropped me off at a hotel outside of town with the understanding that he would show me the famous Patrician sites tomorrow. Unfortunately, after he had pulled away, I was informed at the desk that the hotel was filled already. There I was: without transportation, and without a room, and wondering where and if I would ever find a place to settle in. The manager, however, was friendly, phoned Ballynahinch, a nearby town, and then had one of the bartenders give me a ride to that hotel. I was most appreciative once again of people's generosity toward a perfect stranger.

I am exhausted, but looking forward very much to tomorrow and Father McGuire's tour. It is obvious from the old prints of

Irish monasteries on his walls (like those in my study at home), and his historical interest in the Early Celtic Church that he and I are kindred spirits. My tour of Ireland is quickly coming to a close, and I cannot believe how fast the time has gone. Thank you, Patrick and Brigit, for the past two days.

I watched a BBC program in my room tonight concerning women priests in the Anglican church. Some outstanding women deacons were interviewed who are obviously talented, pastorally competent, and theologically qualified to be priests. I thought of my experience on the island of Iona, off the coast of Scotland, two years ago last summer, when I had gone there in search of solitude, only to find 400 young people from around the world camped out around the restored abbey. Still, they turned out to be a wonderful group, and what I won't forget about the trip was their eucharist at the abbey one night: how natural it seemed to have a woman celebrant leading us in prayer, blessing bread and wine, and passing it to us in Jesus' name. She obviously had the gifts of preaching and celebration, of being able to bring together a very diverse group of people in terms of ages and nationalities, and help us feel like we were a community. I was moved beyond words by the woman's ministry to us. I thought as I left the candlelit church in the drizzling rain that evening of how much we as Roman Catholics are missing by the absence of women at our altars. When it comes to the life of all our Christian communities, none of us is an island, as John Donne reminds us, and even on an island, it seems, we cannot escape how the exclusion of some because they are female or married affects the spiritual well-being of us all.

Friday, October 28

I am back at Maynooth in my own room with my own peat-fire hearth. I walked from the train station after a long, but fascinating train ride from Belfast to Dublin and then another from Dublin to Maynooth. It was a very full day, and just seeing the lighted bell-tower of Maynooth silhouetted against the sky (no moon!) made me sigh with relief.

I cannot quite believe the day! It began at 6:30 when I awakened to a frigid room. As I tried to get back to sleep, the realization came to me that I needed the paycheck from Maynooth for my teaching to get me through the next couple of weeks, and that, after today, the banks would close in Ireland until next Tuesday because of the bank holiday on Monday—and Monday is the day I return to England! In my anxiety, I was reminded of JoAnne and my dilemma on our first visit to Ireland in 1982, and how we had spent a sleepless night on the ferry, wondering if without English money we would be stuck in Liverpool for a day, because the banks were all closed on yet another British bank holiday. (Bankers and bank employees seem to do all right in England and Ireland.) So I got up, showered, had breakfast, and proceeded to make numerous phone calls to Maynooth attempting to reach Ronan, and tell him of my predicament. Thank God for him! When we finally connected he reassured me that my stipend would be cashed and delivered to me in English pounds by the time I returned.

Father McGuire picked me up at 10:30 this morning, and, until he dropped me off at the train station in Belfast at 2:50 P.M. for the 3 o'clock train to Dublin, I was immersed non-stop in Patrician history. I still can't believe all that I saw in such a short amount of time, and I am happy I followed my intuition that I should go to Downpatrick when everyone else I talked to said there was little there to see.

Father McGuire first took me back to Patrick's grave, which I had very briefly visited the night before. He called it, with a smile on his face, "the holiest spot in Ireland," probably remembering Ronan's description of it as "the bogus grave." Then, while Father was off at a parish meeting, I entered the Anglican church on the same grounds as the grave, and received an interesting tour from a woman there. Then I went on to the new Heritage Center, the museum housing so many of the historical artifacts of the Downpatrick area. As I walked into the first exhibit on the ground floor, I almost literally ran into a figure staring down at me from the wall: a life-size drawing of a man from Patrick's *Confessio* named by him "Victoricus," the figure who had appeared in his dream calling him back to Ireland as a missionary. Is that Victoricus the same as the angel Victor whom the ancient *Tripartite Life of St. Patrick* describes as Patrick's *anamchara* or soul friend? If it is, then the original *anamchara* for Patrick was in fact a dream figure, an inner spiritual guide like my "Cuthbert," who came unbidden from the depths, providing significant clues to our deeper Selves and our vocations. Overwhelmed by the same fascination and curiosity as when Cuthbert had first appeared in my dreams, I stood back and stared at this artist's recreation of Patrick's dream figure as he stared back at me. Something resonated within, a dawning awareness. Yes, I thought with wonder, mentoring continues to happen across the centuries: my experience with dreams sheds light on my understanding of Patrick, and his experiences help clarify mine. There is indeed some form of reciprocity in mentoring, a mutuality between soul friends, though separated by time, different cultures, and states of life.

Father McGuire picked me up after I had toured the rest of the exhibits in the museum, and I immediately asked him if he knew whether Victoricus of Patrick's dream was the same as the angel/ *anamchara* Victor of later legends. He thought they were. I was exhilarated, although I want to check the references in the *Tripartite Life* and the *Confessio*, now that I'm back at Maynooth. Because of my own experience with Cuthbert, I understand better why Victoricus would have such meaning for Patrick. And, of course, in that context it makes sense why later generations, appreciative of the guidance human soul friends provide, would come to identify that dream figure as Patrick's soul friend.

This opens another awareness that I have previously overlooked: the ancient Judeo-Christian belief in angels, and how they are often sent as guiding spirits, protecting people from harm and leading them to safety, to new life, to God. What I recall from the *Tripartite Life* is how the angel Victor served in those capacities for Patrick. I have never before thought of angels as soul friends, and since reaching adulthood have always written them off as nonexistent. But now I see that perhaps there is something to the spiritual reality which they represent: the many mysterious ways God cares for us, beyond our wildest expectations. Yes, now I can appreciate much more all those pictures by artists of angels in communion with humankind, and, as portrayed most recently in the Cathedral of Armagh, why early Celtic Christians believed in the existence of these heavenly hosts.

Father McGuire took me next to Saul, outside of Downpatrick, where Patrick supposedly landed the first time as a missionary to Ireland and where, after being led by the angel Victor, he died years later following a vigorous and very effective ministry. We visited the tiny stone church commemorating this event, and then went on to some holy wells, the scene of medieval pilgrimages, according to Father McGuire, when people immersed themselves in the icy waters hoping for a healing of their physical and spiritual ailments. Our next stop (without lunch) was at Inch Abbey, located outside of Downpatrick. Once the site of a Cistercian monastery, the extensive ruins still reveal the traditional beauty and simplicity associated with that religious group, and reminded me of Tintern Abbey in Wales and Rievaulx Abbey in Yorkshire. Finally, as we headed in the direction of Belfast where I was to catch the train, we wended our way down one lonely road after another, across a bridge or two, and eventually stopped at the ancient ruins of one of the earliest Celtic monasteries in all of Ireland: Nendrum on Island Mahee. I climbed out, took pictures with my camera, and traversed as quickly as I could the hills of this now deserted island where the monastery once stood. In some ways, with its graded slopes, it reminded me on a smaller scale of Glastonbury Tor, the site of another early Celtic foundation that became identified with Arthurian myths.

Despite my urge to kill almost anything for food by the time Father McGuire dropped me off at the train station in Belfast, the entire time with him was a marvelous pilgrimage, and I know my teaching, research, and writing will be more vivid and real because I have seen those places with my own eyes.

Spirit of Wisdom, bless that priest who in the midst of many pastoral duties so willingly and happily shared with me an appreciation of common spiritual heritage and a great love of St. Patrick.

As the train left the city of Belfast behind, dark mountains, pastures of grazing sheep, and then a long stretch of seashore could be seen through the windows. The rapidly changing scenes were breath-taking, as my soul is always touched by the power and beauty of the sea, the white-capped breakers crashing against the shore of rock and sand, the strong and powerful surges of the water. I was listening to the tape, "Brendan's Voyage," on my portable player, and the haunting sounds of the pipes and orchestra blended together with the scene outside the train, giving musical expression to the silent music of the sea. Suddenly another wave of sadness came over me, similar to that experienced in the Anglican cathedral of Armagh. I grieved for Ireland and its spiritual and emotional divisions; for myself, that I would soon be leaving this country that I loved as if my own. Yet, as we continued to travel across it, I was struck how much the land itself remained the same, and that, except for seeing less graffiti regarding the IRA on train station walls the closer we got to Dublin, it seemed *one* land, despite all the hatreds and the bloodshed of centuries. It seemed that Ireland should be one nation, not divided into two countries with separate governments. Yet, according to my conversation with Father McGuire in the car, while many might agree with that assessment, most don't believe it will happen in their lifetimes; that unity will not occur until, as the saying goes, "Ten years after I'm dead." That seems to be the human condition: peace eluding us generation after generation, as our children grow up and inherit the same bitterness and hatred of their parents. If only the cycle somehow could be stopped, and ancient wounds healed with the powerful balm of forgiveness.

Still the Irish landscape with its rugged beauty and the fragile globe on which we live speak of unity and the inherent need for making bonds of unity, community with all the nations of this planet—a reality to which Cardinal O'Fiaich alluded yesterday during the Mass when he quoted an Irish proverb,"There is no strength without unity." My prayer this evening as I sit here by my fire is for Ireland, both North and South; for a cessation to the killings which so indiscriminately cut down innocent women and men, children and old people alike. Surely there must be a better way, and not, as Father McGuire says, "Ten years after I'm dead."

Saturday, October 29

The fire is warming my room after a rather brisk, but sunny autumn day in Dublin. I went in this morning on the train, crowded with holiday travelers, and returned in late afternoon by bus (also crowded, but this time I managed to get a seat). I wanted to do some shopping for the last time, and say goodbye to the Irish city that I've come to know so well. I found the tape by the Chieftains, recommended to me by Father McGuire, with the songs of the famous Irish poet and blind harpist, Carolan. I had never heard of the man before Father told me about him, so my Irish education continues, supported by all sorts of people who are possibly not even aware of how helpful they are to "the Yank." While in Dublin, I also found in an antiquarian bookstore two old books on early Irish history, one of which I have been trying to find for years, since it is such a classic, but, as usual, out of print.

The sidewalks in Dublin were crowded with people out enjoying the long weekend with its extra bank holiday on Monday. I strolled through St. Stephen's Green, Dublin's central park area, looked in at "the Bailey" where Leopold and Molly Bloom resided in Joyce's *Ulysses*, and had lunch at Davy Byrne's pub where Joyce used to drink. Again, I wished that JoAnne was with me to enjoy the place and people who came in. Good times are meant to be shared, but I seem able to tolerate being alone more now, possibly because I know that she'll soon be with me. I have learned these months to be alone, to enjoy solitude, to drink deeply of its goodness, but I still yearn to be with her and the boys.

I am writing thank you notes to people here at the college for their hospitality and friendship. My stay here has been so good for me professionally and personally, and I feel a great deal of gratitude for all those who made my visit so worthwhile, especially Ronan and Maria Flood, his secretary in *The Furrow* office. When those letters are finished, I have to read twenty-eight papers from my students. Those should keep me going for the rest of the evening and all day tomorrow.

Sunday, October 30

A beautiful sunny day! Who says it only rains in Ireland? I have noticed, however, since living here that the weather may be responsible for the temperamental extremes associated with the Celts: when it's sunny here, it is glorious and everyone seems most cheerful; when it's gloomy, the dog had better not get in the way.

Right now the campus is very quiet with the students and most of the faculty gone on vacation. I had breakfast with one of the priests and then went for a walk and bought a paper at the corner store. The big news in the papers over the past weeks has been the trial of three Irish young people accused by the British government of conspiring to kill a government official. The mother of one of those convicted is on the faculty here, so there has been real antagonism about the recent verdict sentencing all three of the young people to twenty-five years in prison. Sympathy extends well beyond the campus, however, with most of the public in the Republic of Ireland outraged by a number of ways the trial was handled, the apparently flimsy evidence brought against the accused, and the harsh sentences they received. It seems only to increase the distrust between the Republic and those in the north.

Well, enough of this. On to the mountains of papers that I have to read and grade.

I am struck by the wisdom of one of the seminarians in his paper on prayer and spirituality. Aidan Costello says that there has to be a balance between carrying a heavy workload (i.e., social work) and one's prayer life—or a weak prayer life will result in too great a strain, perhaps even burn-out. "However, if my prayer life is strong and deeply rooted, then I will be better able to carry an equally heavy load of work, to bear the weight of our brothers' and sisters' pain and suffering, because it will not be me carrying the load, but God." His conclusion, of course, has been written before, to the point of sounding platitudinous, but now, after the past year, I realize how much I was trying to do "on a wing and a prayer"—a lot of wing, really, and little prayer. No wonder I felt at times so alone, tired, and depressed.

I am discovering that it is not enough, as a theologian, to lecture about prayer. No, I must pray, for, as the Eastern Orthodox tradition has always affirmed, the vocation of the theologian is rooted in his or her prayer life. The past few months away from home have taught me that in prayer there is a presence of strength, healing, gratitude, and joy, despite any exhaustion, brokenness, or loneliness that may overwhelm us. Solitude is not empty of presence, and silence has the power to speak.

This is my last night in Ireland. I returned from supper and added peat to the fire I'd left, and then lit the candle in front of my "traveling shrine": the hand-carved statues of Brigit and Patrick from Sligo, the picture of "Cuthbert" from the *Book of Durrow*, the icon of Jesus, and Rublev's icon of the Holy Trinity. I turned out my desklamp and sat down in front of the fireplace with the only light coming from the burning peat and the candle on the mantelpiece. I began listening to the haunting music of bagpipes and voices from the tape, "The Pilgrim." As I sat there praying, having consciously put myself in the presence of God, I suddenly became aware that surrounding the figure of my "Cuthbert" from the *Book of Durrow* was a door; yes, that the colored, intricately intertwined Celtic hoops were forming, and surrounding a door back into time, into the time beyond time, into the time and timelessness of God. As I sat there, I began to imagine myself walking through the door and going back, back into time, and, as I journeyed back, I encountered in "the past" many people who dwell in my unconscious, my psyche, my soul.

I was back with David of Wales in the days when he walked the cliffs overlooking the sea and watched the waves come streaming in against the rocks; I was in the small coracle of a boat with Columcille as he crossed the Irish Sea and landed on Iona to begin a new life in his middle years; I was with Patrick as he carried the Christian faith to so many in Ireland, and with Brigit as she lit the sacred fire at Kildare; I was on Inner Farne with Cuthbert, and helped him construct his tiny cell with its window open to air cooled by the sea.

Then the centuries passed, and I was with my ancestors, the Foys, in the cottage in County Mayo as they faced starvation and poverty, and wondered aloud what their options were if they were to survive. Suddenly I was with Grandma Mary as she grew up in her large Irish family in Minnesota, and later, as a mother and grandmother living on a farm in the sweeping prairie loneliness of North Dakota, learned compassion and her tremendous ability to love. Then the scene changed again, in my imagination, and I was with my own father and mother as they grew to adulthood, met, fell in love, and opened their lives and hearts to my brother and sister and me.

Finally, I was with JoAnne, John, and Daniel, reunited once more in a new and different way, our love deepened profoundly by the horrible absence of my being gone. I, in particular, had changed: more deeply respectful of them and their lives as truly sacred, even as I have discovered the past as a sacred thing; no longer taking them for granted or as somehow hindrances to my own vocation as a teacher and writer with professional goals and responsibilities.

Suddenly the whole darkened room was alive with all of their presence, surrounding me in an intimate, awesome, and at times almost frightening way, since the experience itself was so real and beyond the rational categories of the mind. It was an experience of communion: a communion of souls, a communion of saints that will never die because we live together in the power of love and in the living remembrance of God, and everything we do in time, because of God's love, is not lost or forgotten or passed over.

And then I became aware of my icon of Jesus, the one Daniel had kissed so spontaneously as a small child and that has traveled with me wherever I've gone this fall on my pilgrimage. It seemed, as I turned my attention to it, that, although only one of my wisdom figures alongside Brigit, Patrick, and Cuthbert too, Jesus was the one who had led all of us to God, to the realization of God's presence and love; the one who had united all of us together in a living community transcending space and time. He was the one in the Holy Trinity with whom we could all most readily identify because his human journey had intersected each of ours, revealing the sacred dimensions of our own journeys through time. As tears of awe and thanksgiving rose to my eyes, my heart was filled with gratitude at that moment of recognition, and my soul seemed overflowing with the experience of God's goodness.

Seated there in front of the hearth with its rapidly diminishing flames, I came back to my own life and times, realizing that my journeys to Celtic lands over the years were not just for academic research, but on another level were quests in search of soul. Together they mysteriously formed a pilgrimage of the heart that has brought me, in my solitude, face-to-face with my deeper self and my God. And although nothing outwardly has changed, I am not the same, and never will be again.

❖ 7 ❖

PASSAGE INTO LIGHT
November 1-December 26, 1988

The transformation which took place in me
Transformed for me the one unchanging form.
For there within the substance of that light,
Profound and clear, three rings appeared to me
Of colours three, but of one magnitude;
One seemed to be reflected by the other
As rainbow is by rainbow....

Dante, *Paradiso*, Canto 33

Tuesday, November 1, All Saints

I arrived back at St. Theosevia's last night around 8 o'clock, thoroughly exhausted. Yesterday began well with the sun out again and a wonderful breakfast of eggs and sausages in the priests' dining room at Maynooth. I packed the rest of my belongings and Ronan came to say goodbye. Then Leo Larkin, one of the seminarians I had taught, picked me up and took me to the airport. On the way, in the course of our conversation, he unexpectedly asked me what I thought of the contemporary church.

The question caught me by surprise, and at first irritated me with its bluntness. What could I honestly tell this young seminarian without perhaps disillusioning or hurting him? So young, what did he know of life and the hurt that comes from the institution's darker side? I decided, however, to speak honestly, and surprised myself by what came forth.

"I can't deny," I said, "that I am having serious problems with aspects and actions of the institutional church that often seem opposed to greater lay participation, as well as the greater inclusiveness of women. I also don't think it helps the cause of ecumenism at all when this same church treats with contempt and even condemns those within it who may differ in their theological views. But," I added, "I love the church and I am hopeful of its future. I say that because over the past months here, in England, and in Wales I have met so many good people, lay and ordained, who are struggling as I am. All of us are trying to discern answers to some basic questions: what does God want of us; how do we pray well; what parts of our spiritual heritage can provide guidance for our daily lives; how can we foster a spirituality that will bring about greater unity among our churches? Again and again, through the friendships that I've made, I've experienced new hope and a renewed sense of faith in God." Then, glancing over for a moment to look directly at Leo, I found myself saying with conviction, "I believe that the People of God, this church of which we are such an important part, the one we encounter in our daily relationships with our families, friends, and colleagues, will continue to grow strong, sometimes despite the institution's lack of response to pastoral, sacramental, and spiritual needs; sometimes precisely because of its opposition."

As I talked (and, really, overheard myself speak), I realized how much that virtue of hope that the ancients equated with strength of soul had come back into my life since leaving the States in August. I was not just saying these things to make Leo and myself feel good; no, I believed them. People are basically good and loving; they will continue to seek out God in their good times and bad, as God will continue to seek them out to comfort and give them courage. That has been true, I thought as we continued our drive, of my pilgrimage this fall.

I remembered Manus in the kitchen at St. Theosevia's that first night, offering me part of his meal; my trip down the curving roads of Wales as Donald uttered yet another, "Oh, now that's a pleasant view!" Savas taking me out for dinner and advising me what to read; Benedicta welcoming me into her study and life of scholarship; Helen Columba telling me that spirituality is much more than what you find in books. I recalled the Hebblethwaites' kitchen with Margaret putting food on the table while Peter shooed away the cat; the smiling faces of Sr. Brigette at Littlemore and of Ulrich, the Birmingham cab driver who took me on a free tour of the city at his expense.

Still other faces and holy places came to mind: Alison, Kajetan, Nigel, Reverend Bill, Michael, Peggy, and the rest of the Marygate community on Holy Island who gave new meaning to the word "hospitality"; Brendan O'Malley who mirrored my own passion for Celtic spirituality and thirst for solitude; Mary and Antony Lewis, Bishop Verney and those at the Skreen who, through their acceptance of my sins, moved aside the clouds that concealed a God worthy of trust; Val and Wyn and their sons who took in strangers at St. David's, humans and animals alike; the Sligo woodcarver, Michael, who told me about his love of Celtic pagan mythology and the heritage of the early Celtic saints, and, of course, Eithne, his long-suffering wife who gave me a new perspective on what it might be like to be married to a Celtic "enthusiast"; Ronan, Enda, Padraig, Maria, Betty, and all the priests and students at Maynooth who, like the earliest inhabitants of Irish monasteries, made a traveling scholar feel at home; Ben Kimmerling, Gerry Mangan, and the lay people at Emmaus House who shared with me their own desire for a truly inclusive church; Cardinal O'Fiaich at Armagh and Father McGuire, my guide at Downpatrick, who made my anxious trip to Northern Ireland so worthwhile by helping me encounter firsthand more of my Irish inheritance.

Yes, I thought, they have all contributed a great deal to my pilgrimage and search for soul. Along with the guidance I received from my dream figures, from Cuthbert, and Grandma Mary too, all have helped me find what the American Transcendentalist Ralph Waldo Emerson describes as a "new angle of vision": seeing "the same old things" in a new way, from another perspective, a new perspective of gratitude and compassion.

Of course, I knew this all before I moved to Oxford: that God is good, and that the People of God, made in God's image, share profoundly in the goodness of all creation, despite our conflicts over religious and ecclesial realities that mean a great deal to so many of us. I knew this, but now, I have rediscovered that reality—and that conviction—at a deeper level of consciousness.

We drove on to the airport, and, as Leo spoke in response to my comments, it was my turn to be surprised by his evident lack of naivety, and by what he hoped for the church regarding lay participation, women's inclusion, and pastoral leadership.

When we arrived at the airport, I checked my suitcases which weighed a ton, filled, as they were, with my research notes, duplicated pages, and books. Then Leo and I had a quick hamburger together before saying goodbye. I boarded the British Airways plane, settled in my seat, and then waited...and waited... and waited. It was as if Ireland refused to let me go. We sat for close to an hour on the runway, only to be told that due to "mechanical difficulties" we must deplane. Then we sat for another hour in the airport lounge, received new tickets on Air Lingus, reboarded, and settled back in our seats. The voice of the new captain came on the loudspeaker: "I am very sorry, but we're having mechanical problems, so we'll have to taxi back to the terminal." Most of us couldn't believe our ears, and thought at first that this must be some kind of bad Halloween joke. It wasn't. We waited for yet another hour on the ground, and then finally took off. What was suppose to have been an early afternoon flight from Ireland, however, now had us landing in England at night, and I found myself with all my luggage trying to find, in the pitch-black darkness outside the airport, a bus back to Oxford that wasn't already filled.

When I had boarded one, the hour ride went quickly, and there was a taxi that appeared shortly after the bus arrived at the station in pouring rain. It was so good to cross the bridge back into Oxford, and see Magdalen's tower and spires once again. I went out for a late pub supper, and found Donald waiting for me upon my return. He wanted to know all about my adventure, and over glasses of port I recounted the highlights of my trip to Ireland. He was genuinely enthused. Ciaran, back from Toronto, came in, as we were talking, with his "traveler" friend, Michael. Then I went off to bed, after reading a stack of letters from my family and friends in the States that Savas had given me. It was good to hear from everyone; to know that they seemed to be missing me as I was missing them.

This morning a letter arrived from JoAnne with news from home. I can't wait to be with her in Italy and then to see the boys again! I boxed up my books and Donald and Ciaran gave me a ride to Blackwells' warehouse which packaged and sent all of them for a reasonable fee. Then I went and bought a pair of walking shoes, since I had left my old and tired pair at Maynooth, and met Savas at Heroes for lunch. I enjoyed the chance to tell him about Ireland, and to get caught up on his studies and research.

The weather, as I walked around Oxford today, was beautiful. I passed the Sheldonian with its wonderful Greek and Roman faces, the Bodleian, the Bridge of Sighs, St. Mary's church, all the places I love. It felt so good to be back again, and, although I will be leaving soon, I know that I will return someday, as Donald says I will. Perhaps with my sons next time, certainly for a shorter stay than the one I've been priviledged to have this fall.

I had an excellent discussion on my trip to Ireland with Benedicta this afternoon. I started by telling her of my teaching and research experiences, and then of my visit to Northern Ireland. I mentioned how much I appreciated the artistic beauty of the Roman Catholic cathedral in Armagh that expresses so well the spiritual heritage of Celtic Christians. She was intrigued with my description of the beautiful mosaics that tell the story of Brigit, including the scene of a bishop placing his hands over Brigit's head in blessing, in recognition of her spiritual power. Then I launched into my discovery about the Irish concept of time: how early and medieval Celtic Christians seemed to disregard time in a chronological sense, and in the legends, lives, and stories of the saints make them contemporaries of Jesus and Mary, or contemporaries with each other even though historically they could have never met. They seemed to be saying that relationships of depth transcend those chronological differences, and in many ways stand outside of time. This I knew already from my own relationships with significant mentors and friends, but it was enlightening to see how earlier Christians had similar feelings about these spiritual friendships; how their experiences helped clarify my own. Unlike modern Western peoples who seem to be constantly rushing about to avoid the passage of time, the early Celts, I told Benedicta, seemed to have another awareness, epitomized in the old Irish saying, "When God made time, he made plenty of it."

Somehow this discussion about time led to my telling her about my prayer experience the last night at Maynooth. My going back into time, beyond time, confirmed the belief I already had that in some ways time and space are transcended in the power of friendship and love. That's precisely the way many Christians can experience Christ as so contemporary with us, because we are in direct relationship with him as a wisdom figure, teacher, and soul friend, despite being separated by centuries from the "historical" person of Christ. Benedicta listened attentively, and then said: "Perhaps the Reformation in its desire to be free of past customs was in some ways responsible for our thinking of time only in chronological terms, as if what is past is behind us, and that we need not have any further relationship with it. This attitude was certainly not characteristic of the Middle Ages when there was a vivid sense that we were all connected in the vast communion of saints. As Peter Brown says in his book, *The Cult of the Saints*, people thought that they already had a personal relationship with the saints, and that when they went on pilgrimage to the shrines, they could deepen that relationship."

"Yes," I thought outloud, "that has been my experience the past months when I went to places associated with Newman, Cuthbert, David, and Patrick, and on previous visits over the years to Glendalough, Kildare, Iona, Melrose, Rievaulx, Norwich, and Lewis's home here in Oxford. I have felt, even though they have been dead for years or centuries, as if I have made direct contact with them, and that somehow that meeting them on their own sacred territory took the form of a personal encounter with them that changed me in unexpected and at times profound ways."

"That has been my experience too," she said, "most recently on my visits to Bede's monastery at Jarrow for research on my book." She paused, and added: "Yes, despite the Reformation, despite the Enlightenment, many of us in this modern age, including many scientists, are now beginning to rethink our concepts of time, and the restrictive categories of time in which our modern culture has had us think."

As I drank the last of my tea that she had offered me when I came in, and then prepared to leave, Benedicta said with a knowing smile, "I too, as you did your last night in Ireland around the fire, have discovered in prayer a living, powerful presence transcending the rational. To call upon the saints is to sense immediately their care and interest in us; to experience that they are there by our side *right now!*"

Holy One, on this feast of All Saints, thank you for all those holy women and men, ordinary and extraordinary in my life; all those who have touched my life in conscious and unconscious ways, revealing your love and your goodness. And thank you today especially for Benedicta, Helen Columba, Donald, and Savas who have taught me so much during my time here in Oxford.

Wednesday, November 2, All Souls Day

I began this somber, overcast morning with prayer, thinking of all of us poor souls, dead and living, in need of God's care.

Yesterday at breakfast Donald pointed out a passage from Peter O'Dwyer's book which I had loaned him on the Celi De, the eighth-century reform movement in Ireland that emphasized in its spirituality the value of a soul friend. I think the wisdom of one early Irish soul friend, abbess Samthann, agrees with what I learned this fall on my own pilgrimage:

A certain teacher named Daircellach came to the virgin (Abbess Samthann) and said to her: "I propose to lay aside study and give myself to prayer." To whom she replied: "What then can give your mind stability that it wander not," she said, "if you neglect spiritual study?" The teacher continued, "I wish to go across the sea on pilgrimage," said he. She replied, "If God could not be found on this side of the sea we would indeed journey across. Since, however, God is nigh unto all who call upon Him, we are under no obligation to cross the sea. The kingdom of heaven can be reached from every land."

Later Samthann adds: "The distance to heaven is the same from every end of the earth and if a person comes close to God he cannot be far from home."

I took Donald's advice yesterday and decided not to travel to Little Gidding or Cornwall as I had hoped to do before leaving England. "Save those places for another visit," he said, "and use the little time you have left to put your research together, and write as much as you can on your book." He's right.

Going back over some of my journal this morning, I came across my description of the dream of the tornadoes and Grandma Mary on St. Cuthbert's Day this spring, and almost broke into tears. I hadn't fully realized how much anxiety I have been living with, especially when I heard that there were those trying to prevent me from teaching and receiving tenure. All this autumn I have felt the dark cloud of dread lifting, a cloud that has colored my perspective on life and God. I meant what I said to Leo on the way to the airport and what so many others, like Etty Hillesum in her diaries, have said: people really are basically good, and so often they only await a smile and a smile is returned. Again this sounds platitudinous, but sometimes, I am becoming aware, there is great truth in platitudes. They so often express a folk wisdom based upon the experience of numerous lives over the centuries.

Friday, November 4

This morning, while reading a book on Irish traditions, I came across this poetry from an eighth-century work in the *Book of Leinster:*

> A breathing branch that flowers in spring,
> A vessel brimmed with honey sweet,
> A precious ruby beyond price—
> Such he that follows Christ's own feet.
>
> The man that does Christ's heavenly will,
> He is the sun that warms the year,
> God's image through his heart doth pass,
> He is a glass of crystal clear.

I spent all day yesterday writing, as I did the day before. I would rather be out and about, savoring my last days in Oxford, but I want to get to certain material and write about it before I leave and have to begin the process of re-collecting my data and thoughts all over again when I get home. Perhaps it is staying in my room all day and having to concentrate so much on my research material, but I am feeling more and more anticipation for my reunion with JoAnne and, after Italy, with my sons. Music seems to help. I purchased a tape at Blackwells Music Store of Vivaldi's "Four Seasons," which brought back fond memories of the night at the Sheldonian with the Griffins. (I see Bill's book on C.S. Lewis in all the bookstores now.) The tape is well done, and through its beauty I am discovering once again good music's capacity to heal and soothe the soul.

Last night I went to a talk next door at the Orthodox church given by Bishop Kallistos Ware on the subject of the eucharist. His presentation with its references to Blake and Wordsworth and even Charles Williams, C.S. Lewis's good friend, was most worthwhile. Bishop Ware is a very good speaker who has the ability of an actor to put himself into the words, while using expressive and dramatic gestures at the appropriate times. The candlelit church with its many beautiful icons made the presentation especially moving. A large number of people obviously thirsting for wisdom and the holy life, as so many are in the United States, turned out to hear him.

I am about to leave for an entire day at the computer center. I hope it is not too busy and noisy, as I need to concentrate. Thank you, Holy One, for your goodness in all things.

Sunday, November 6

Opening the curtains this morning, I beheld a view of Oxford that any poet or romantic would appreciate. Before me in the backyard was a thick, gray fog, its wisps of mist covering the garden, filtering between the trees now almost barren of their leaves. In the distance, I could barely make out the faint outline of roofs and spires. It's no wonder that writers associate this city with a mystical feeling, and that autumn is considered the most beautiful of Oxford seasons. Gerard Manley Hopkins's poetry came to mind as I beheld the sight outside my window: "The world is charged with the grandeur of God." This place truly is, as he says so pleasingly in his "Duns Scotus's Oxford," a "towery city and branchy between towers, cuckoo-echoing, bell-swarmed, lark-charmed, rook-racked, river-rounded."

Last night there were sounds of fireworks in honor of Guy Fawkes Day, and a shower of falling fireworks lit up the sky in front of St. Theosevia's as I walked back from evensong at Magdalen College. I had gone there in the early evening to see if any

eucharistic services might be open to the public today, only to discover that evensong in the chapel was about to begin. Candlelit
choir stalls greeted a group of us as we walked into the chapel,
and soon the choir of mostly young boys joined us in their stalls.
One boy, in particular, reminded me of Daniel, and another of
John, and tears came to my eyes in anticipation of seeing them
again. The service, with its prayers, readings, psalms, and a closing selection from Palestrina, was wonderful, and had special
meaning because this was the place where C.S. Lewis once worshipped and the college where he once taught.

Lewis,
I have been avoiding you the past months, fully aware of
what I was doing. Unlike previous visits, I have not gone in
search of the places that I associate with you and your ministries. For a reason. I wanted to be free of you, as I have wanted to be free of Robert Kennedy, no longer comparing myself
to the two of you, but beginning to appreciate who I am
with my own gifts and limitations. This pilgrimage to foreign shores has helped me a great deal. I am becoming more
accepting of myself, and, with that recognition, something
has changed in yours and my relationship this fall. Despite
your obvious talents, Lewis, I no longer put you on a pedes-
tal or, perhaps more importantly, need to do so. You have
become much more of a friend, a person who journeys with
me as my companion, rather than a distant figure whom I
must emulate. It was knowing this that made the evening
prayer service last night all the more special. Thank you for
your presence in my life, and for your continuing friendship.

Yesterday was a full day of presentations at St. Theosevia's on
the theme of spiritual fatherhood in the Russian tradition: by Bishop Kallistos Ware, Fr. Basil Osborne (one of the pastors of the
Orthodox community next door) and Militza Zernov, who welcomed me my first day in Oxford. Donald introduced the speakers,

and immediately broadened the term "spiritual fatherhood" to include spiritual motherhood as well. When Bishop Ware began his talk, he stated that in addition to the Eastern Orthodox ordained *startzy*, the tradition very much included lay monks and nuns, as well as "ordinary" laity. While Fr. Basil spoke about the history and *startzy* specifically related to the Monastery of Optino and Militza spoke of one *staretz* in particular, St. Seraphim (the favorite of Sr. Helen Columba), Bishop Ware traced what he called a "pattern" in the history of the spiritual guide in Russia.

According to him, the ministry of the *staretz* is essentially "charismatic," that is, arising from the experience of being called by God and by others, rather than a clearly-defined function within the institutional framework of the church, the office of the priest. Though the *staretz's* ministry will include confessional encounters, his or her gift to the community is primarily that of giving advice, "not only at confession, but on many other occasions." He or she is recognized for the gifts of discernment and listening, and these charisms are recognized as such by the people themselves. Bishop Ware made it clear that "the initiative comes, as a rule, not from the master but from the disciples"; in other words, the vocation is often discerned by others first, by their calling it forth (as in the desert tradition when people came in search of the spiritual father or mother for guidance, often against the guide's own desires).

Bishop Ware also made it clear that, although the *startzy* are not necessarilly ordained, some preparation is needed for their ministries.

The classic pattern for this ministerial formation, according to him, consists of flight and return, as can be seen in the lives of the desert hermit, St. Antony of Egypt, and (wouldn't you know?) St. Seraphim of Sarov. "A person must learn to be alone," Ware said, "to listen in one's heart to the wordless speech of the Spirit, and to discover the truth about oneself and God. Then the *staretz's* word to others will be a word of power, because it is a word of silence." The bishop continued. "The real journey of the *staretz* is not spatially into the desert, but spiritually into the heart. The moment we begin to acknowledge our powerlessness to heal the wounds of humanity solely by our own efforts, that is the time we enter upon the path of the *staretz*, when we seek with humble sincerety to enter into the secret chamber of the heart." Prayer, then, is of utmost importance in the life of every *staretz*, a form of prayer that takes others' burdens into one's heart, solitude, and, yes, soul. Quoting Dostoyevsky in *The Brothers Karamazov*, Bishop Ware said: "A *staretz* is one who takes your soul, your will, unto his soul and his will." Then the bishop added: "It is not enough for the *staretz* to offer advice. He or she is also required to take up the soul of one's spiritual children into one's own soul, their life into one's own life. It is the task of praying for them." When the person has learned all of this firsthand, most often in solitude, then he or she is ready to return, to give of himself or herself in a ministry that touches other lives and other souls.

The more the bishop talked, the more enthused I became. I began to see how all of this touched upon the research I have been doing into the Celtic soul-friend tradition, as well as the emergence of lay spiritual guides today.

Doesn't everyone's discernment of vocation often follow the same pattern of separation and return, what Gretchen Berg and others like Joseph Campbell call the stages of separation, liminality, and reintegration? Isn't the soul friend tradition all about the reality of the soul and those relationships of great intimacy between people? Isn't a second flowering of spiritual guides today, so many who are lay people, related to their discernment of vocation at the grassroots, the encouragement from friends and ordinary folk to pursue their thirst for spirituality and hopes of becoming spiritual guides? Isn't this what my research into C.S. Lewis's life and ministries several years ago taught me, how one does not have to be ordained to be an effective spiritual guide? The gift in itself has its origins from the creative, Holy Spirit of Wisdom, who is often years ahead of any institutional response or recognition.

Most important, I realized how much Bishop Ware's and my own experiences and insights resonated with each other's. Wasn't this what I have been learning over the past months here in Celtic lands as I entered into a solitude I had not fully expected and learned to pray as I never had before? Isn't this what my midlife transition has been teaching me the past three years: the importance of paying attention to one's heart and listening for the traces of God's call, not only in conversations with friends, but in dreams and with the use of the imagination? What's more, isn't this the knowledge that I have been given in my liminal state this fall, separated as I've been from family and kin: the need to pray continuously for people, as my Grandma Mary always did, especially in her last years? Haven't I also learned in this unexpected solitude the need to acknowledge my limitations in being able to effect major changes in church and society on my own?

Bishop Ware was the most dynamic of the three speakers (and obviously the one who touched me the most), but all of them provided, from differing perspectives, insights that are worthy of continuing reflection. Tonight I was reading an article Bishop Ware gave me which he had written, and I came across a quote from the great *staretz*, St. Seraphim, that the saint had had inscribed on his tombstone when he died: "When I am dead, come to me at my grave, and the more often, the better. Whatever is on your soul, whatever may have happened to you, come to me as when I was alive and, kneeling on the ground, cast all your bitterness upon my grave. Tell me everything and I shall listen to you, and all the bitterness will fly away from you. And as you spoke to me when I was alive, do so now. For I am living, and I shall be forever." I remembered the continuing presence of Grandma Mary as I have journeyed this fall, and the insights given by my relationship with Cuthbert, a saint who has been dead for over 1300 years.

I had a farewell drink with Donald before retiring last night. He is leaving tomorrow for the States and a series of talks that he'll give in Boston, Massachusetts, and Albany, New York. He seems excited about going, and also finding out more about the first Episcopalian woman priest nominated to be a bishop. While that decision among U.S. Episcopalians has caused a great deal of stir in England among Anglicans, I told him that many Roman Catholics in the States are happy that the Episcopalians are taking the initiative on this essential issue of ministerial inclusiveness. I will miss his warm smile, his enthusiasm for Christianity's rich and very diverse spiritual heritage, and especially our conversations at the breakfast table or in the evenings over a glass of port. His friendship, of course, I carry with me, one that I'm confident will deepen in time and memory.

I am counting the days and hours until I see JoAnne again. Please, Holy One, give her a safe flight over, and keep our boys safe while we're gone.

I hear the bells next door from the Orthodox church calling people to prayer. I too must leave for worship. I plan to have tea later this afternoon with Columba Stewart, a Benedictine from St. John's Abbey in Collegeville, and then go as Savas's guest to Pembroke College for dinner with the students and staff tonight.

Monday, November 7

I spoke with JoAnne and John yesterday. Daniel was still asleep. JoAnne is looking forward to Italy, as am I, and we'll meet at Heathrow airport this Thursday morning. I asked John about Halloween, and if Greg and Bobbie had taken him trick-or-treating, and he said, "Yes, but you'll take me next year, won't you, Dad?" I needed to hear that: that he wants me to be involved in his life, and that, despite my being gone, he still loves me. JoAnne also said that John told her that he wants to wrestle and pillow fight with me when I get home.

Holy One, thank you for my wife and children, gifts that my heart for so many years longed for. You are a loving God who knows the secrets of our hearts far more and sooner than we know them ourselves. I want to be a better parent and husband when I return, more centered in the life of my family, and more present and responsive to them. Please help me, Holy One, set and keep my priorities, making you and them my primary ones.

Dinner last night at Pembroke was right out of a Victorian novel. All of the students were dressed in their black robes (which they also have to wear to classes), and stood waiting for the professors and their wives, dressed in tuxedoes and beautiful dresses, to file by on their way to the head table. They had been in the college faculty lounge for sherry beforehand, Savas whispered as they walked by. "Graduate students are invited there once or twice a year," he said, "if they're good...." One of the professors rang a bell to get our attention and to obtain silence, and, after he had led us in prayer, we all sat down and began a clamorous meal. I sat with Savas and other graduate students, a number of whom were from the States, one from Australia, and another from Japan. We discussed the various topics they were studying and the political situation in the States, while the portraits of famous academicians stared down at us from the walls as the din from our voices rose to the high ceilings above. Then, before I knew it, the bell had rung again and we were dismissed into the night.

Monday evening: I spent this morning writing more on the soul friend book, and then went to the Bodleian for some last-minute research into passages on the angel Victor in the *Life of St. Patrick* that contains the earliest legends of Patrick, written by the monk Muirchu. I wasn't imagining things. There are definite references to the Early Celtic Churches equating the angel Victor with Victoricus, the dream figure who came to Patrick and helped him discern, after his escape from Ireland as a slave, that he was being called back as a missionary. According to Patrick's Confession, no. 23:

> And next a few years later I was in Britain among my parents who had received me for their son and earnestly requested me that I should now after all the troubles which I

had experienced never leave them, and it was there that I saw in a vision of the night a man coming apparently from Ireland whose name was Victoricus, with an uncountable number of letters, and he gave me one of them and I read the heading of the letter which ran, "The Cry of the Irish," and while I was reading aloud the heading of the letter I was imagining that at that very moment I heard the voice of those who were by the Wood of Voclut which is near the Western Sea, and this is what they cried, as with one voice, "Holy boy, we are asking you to come and walk among us again," and I was struck deeply to the heart and I was not able to read any further and at that I woke up.

According to the scholar R.P.C. Hanson, in his book, *The Life and Writings of the Historical Saint Patrick,* "Victoricus is clearly the origin of the guardian angel Victor who looks after Patrick in an obliging way in the later stories about him." It is this same Victor that is identified in "Notes on Fiacc's Hymn," published in the *Tripartite Life,* as "Patrick's soul friend, and he is the common angel of the Gael. As Michael of the Jews so is Victor of the Scots (Irish)." Like Jung's Philemon, the helping spirits of the shamans, as well as the daemon or genius the Greeks and Romans equated with the soul, Victor was Patrick's soul friend, and thus, through Patrick, soul friend and companion to the entire Irish race.

What is intriguing to me now, in retrospect, is how my own "Cuthbert" figure in my dreams was in many ways responsible for calling me back to Ireland and the other lands of the Celtic saints, the one who intensified and in many ways clarified my pursuit of soul, of the spiritual tradition of the soul friend, and of my Celtic roots.

The other quotation that I found about St. Brigit from the *Book of Lismore* makes the mosaics in the cathedral at Armagh even more interesting:

Brigit and certain virgins along with her went to take the

veil from Bishop Mel in Telcha Mide. Happy was he to see them. For humility Brigit stayed so that she might be the last to whom a veil should be given. A fiery pillar rose from her head to the roof-ridge of the church. Then said Bishop Mel: "Come, O holy Brigit, that a veil may be sained on thy head before the other virgins." It came to pass then, through the grace of the Holy Ghost, that the form of ordaining a bishop was read out over Brigit. Mac-Caille said, that a bishop's order should not be conferred on a woman. Said Bishop Mel: "No power have I over this matter. That dignity hath been given by God unto Brigit, beyond every (other) woman." Wherefore the men of Ireland from that time to this give episcopal honour to Brigit's successor.

Ah, if only more bishops and the pope himself might begin to see, as did Bishop Mel, how the fiery power of the Holy Spirit has already called many women to full-time ministry and priesthood.

I stopped off at Tweeds for my last scone, jam, and clotted cream, and a last sweep of Blackwells before my impending departure. Walking at dusk from High Street to Broad Street past St. Edmund's, the oldest surviving medieval college hall off Queen's Lane, and then down the winding lane toward the Bridge of Sighs with the lights of the Radcliffe Camera and the Bodleian peeking through the mist, I was once again struck by the mysterious grandeur of Oxford. The sky was pink and blue in the pale haze of autumn light, and, as students, emerging from the dark, flew by on their bikes and disappeared into the shadows, I suddenly felt caught up once again in an experience that is hard to describe. It was as if I had been in Oxford before, centuries ago, and that I was back again in quest of wisdom.

I am grateful, Holy One, for this tremendous gift of vivid experiences that I will always carry with me. Sr. Columba was right: this time away has had an effect on me that I could barely imagine when I originally made my plans. I will miss being here, but somehow this time away has left a lasting imprint.

I listened to the Vaughn Williams's tape tonight before turning out the light. His music, combined with the poetry of the seventeenth-century Anglican poet and pastor George Herbert, has a power and beauty that is indescribably rich:

Love Bade Me Welcome

Love bade me welcome; yet my soul drew back
Guilty of dust and sin.
But quick-eyed Love, observing me grow slack
From my first entrance in.
Drew nearer to me sweetly questioning
If I lacked anything.

A guest, I answered, worthy to be here:
Love said, You shall be he.
I, the unkind, ungrateful? Ah, my dear.
I cannot look on thee.
Love took my hand and smiling did reply.
Who made the eyes but I?

Truth, Lord, but I have marred them; let my shame
Go where it doth deserve.
And know you not, says Love, who bore the blame?
My dear, then I will serve.
You must sit down, says Love, and taste my meat.
So I did sit and eat.

From *The Call:*

Come, my Joy, my Love, my Heart!
Such a joy, as none can move:

Such a Love, as none can part:
Such a Heart, as joys in love.

And from *Easter:*

Rise, heart: thy Lord is risen. Sing His praise
Without delay.

Yes! Listening to those lyrics, I recognized myself and what I
have experienced this fall in Oxford, Lindisfarne, the Skreen, St.
David's, Maynooth. Yes, Holy One, and I am grateful for so many
manifestations of your love.

Wednesday, November 9

I awoke with the news of George Bush's presidential victory.
Savas and I had watched the returns until early this morning, so I
was not surprised. I do feel depressed: another four years of ignoring the poor and homeless, while Dan Quayle waits in the
wings! It is frightening to think about, and so I am telling myself
not to think about it and not become preoccupied. Life must go
on. If this journey has taught me anything, it is that although nations and institutions will often resist change at any price, change
and conversion can occur on a local level, within our communities, within our families, within ourselves. Centering our lives on
God is cause for gratitude and hope.

Yesterday I met with Benedicta for tea and our last time together. I brought with me the hand-carved statues of Brigit and Patrick from Sligo, and she seemed intrigued by the workmanship
and portrayal of them as figures linked with pagan Celtic mythology. As we talked about my research this fall, and how quickly
the time has flown by, it began to sink in that we would no longer
be meeting on a regular basis. I have valued her comments and
critique of my writing, but most especially her friendship, and I
will miss those opportunities to connect with her on such a fre-
quent basis face-to-face. Benedicta also seemed to have enjoyed

our time together, for as I was leaving she graciously offered to continue to read and critique my work if I sent it to her after I return to the States. We embraced and said goodbye, and I left her there in her study sitting quietly, preparing for yet another student of history.

I spent most of today running about doing errands and trying to fit everything into two suitcases and a briefcase! I have much more duplicated material than I realized, so things are very cramped. I hope the one big suitcase shuts tomorrow! Tomorrow—I can't believe it! I will be leaving Oxford. I am tired right now and anticipating the return home, but I know I will miss greatly the friends I have made here in Oxford. I called and spoke briefly with JoAnne about the election results. Yes, last night she had had another party, small, quiet, and, considering the election results, subdued. I can't wait to see her, and I hope that our time together will be like (as Sr. Helen Columba said to me) "a second honeymoon."

This afternoon I managed to break away from packing to take the bus to Fairacres for one last visit. I had a wonderful tea with Sr. Columba for about an hour. She asked me about Ireland and I told her stories about Michael and Eithne Quirke at Sligo, the many nights by the hearth, my experience in the Long Room at Trinity College, and my last night in Ireland by the fire. She is a wonderful woman with many insights, and I feel very much as if I have known her for years. She certainly has become, like Donald and Benedicta, an important mentor on this journey of mine into Celtic history.

This time she surprised me once again with new information about the Celts. We were discussing how both of us have felt "grounded" in such holy places as Iona when she said that this was probably because they were "thin places." "Thin places? I've never heard the term," I said.

"It refers to those locations where there seems to be only a thin veil between the present and the past," she told me with a smile. "It's as if we step back into time and perhaps only for a moment get a peek into that reality."

I couldn't believe my ears! So that was what I had experienced at various times over the past three years or more on my journeys to Celtic lands: on my first visit to Glendalough, Iona, Holy Island, and, yes, most recently in Oxford the other night walking alone through the fog. So there's a name for this encounter with a reality that transcends our minds and ordinary faculties!

"I think it happened to me," she continued, "for the first time on Iona. I had gone there on holiday for a brief visit, and was so moved by the place that I decided to stay. So I got a job as secretary of the community. One day, as I sat at my typewriter, I happened to look up and glance out the window. I spied a young Scot in kilts standing on the rocks, and it was then, quick as a flash, that I felt as if I was transported through some sort of door back into time, and that I was with a whole people from the past." At this she became more animated. "I thought immediately that I was with the Children of Israel." She paused, and seemed to wonder aloud, "I don't know why."

I thought for a moment, and then remembered something I had read while doing my research. "That's really interesting," I told her, "for that's how the ancient Celtic Christians sometimes described themselves, as the lost tribe of Israel. And of course the two races have much in common: they both respect and value family, tribal identity, and especially relationships of friendship."

She seemed intrigued and happy at this new bit of information, as was I at the new term "thin places" that she had given me. I told her how much I had learned this fall, and how appreciative I was of her taking time from a very busy schedule to be with me. "You were right, Columba," I said, "about the effect Oxford might have on me. I have learned here and at the other places I visited so much more than I had ever imagined I might. Thank you for being such an important part of my learning experience."

"Before you leave," she said, "I want to pray with you and have us perform an old Celtic ritual between friends." She had me stand, and reaching up to my forehead, signed it with the sign of the cross, and then invited me to do the same for her. "It is a simple gesture," she explained, "asking God's blessing and help for each friend until they meet again." We parted with a warm embrace, and as I walked toward the bus stop, I was filled with amazement at who comes into our lives when we most need them.

Thank you, Holy One, for the many ways you have manifested your love the past three months. Continue to teach me to pray, and to always live, as George Herbert expresses in a prayer of his own, with a grateful heart.

Friday, November 11, Rome

It is so good to be with JoAnne again, loving her in the old way, and yet in a new way of greater depth—brought about by our separation. Peggy was right when she told me on Lindisfarne that sometimes it's good for a husband and wife to be apart, that relationships can be strengthened by the mutual absence.

JoAnne and I met, as planned, at Heathrow Airport, outside of London. Both of us were excited about the upcoming trip to Italy, and spent the time at lunch getting caught up on more recent happenings in our lives, and our plans for our vacation together. Then we flew out (on another delayed flight due to "mechancial difficulties"), landed in Rome, took a bus from the airport, and found a decent but fairly inexpensive hotel. For dinner, we walked to a nearby restaurant that was filled with Italians enjoying their night out. This time I could be appreciative of their happiness, rather than feeling lonely or depressed or resentful that there was no one sitting and conversing with me. JoAnne seemed happy too, pleased that she had survived the last few months alone, and that we had this time to relax together.

Today we walked to the Spanish Steps, toured Hadrian's Tomb, walked to the Trevi Fountains, and had an afternoon ice cream cone at the Piazza Navona where our group, a year ago during the Synod on the Laity, had had such a memorable time. We also walked what seemed like miles to the Pantheon, only to find its massive doors had just been closed for the night. This evening, we took a cab to the Columbus Hotel. I had wanted to take JoAnne there since discovering it a year ago. In the quiet and elegant restaurant located on the second floor overlooking a garden, I took out the ring I had purchased in Oxford a few days ago, in a shop on High Street not far from the University Church, St. Mary's. "I want you to have this," I told her, "for all you did while I was gone, but especially for all you are in my life." As she opened the box, I added, "I know words aren't enough, but I'm sorry for all those times I didn't show my appreciation; for all those times I was stubborn or hard to live with; for all the times I've been gone." She was surprised by this unexpected gift, probably more so by my words. "Let's try to be happy," she said smiling, "not just tonight, but from now on...."

I definitely think that it's time for me to return home. JoAnne said tonight at dinner that in a test in religion at school, John, when asked if the church was "the People of God," answered "No," and when asked who teaches him about God, he said, "my mother."

Sunday, November 13

We're in Florence, and back at Mario's, the place we stayed on our honeymoon almost ten years ago. I can't believe it! The place has been redone, and although we don't have a room with a view (our window overlooks an alley), we do have a wonderful king-size bed and our own bathroom! "Someday," I told JoAnne, "we'll also have a view."

This morning, after settling in at Mario's, we went for a walk to the heart of the city: the Duomo, the famous cathedral with its reddish-orange tiled roofs, the baptistry whose beautiful bronze doors were made by Ghiberti, and the elegant campanile with its bells ringing on the quarter-hour. We went in for another visit and, as we walked slowly around the huge interior, I saw, as if for the first time, the famous fifteenth-century fresco of Dante by Domenico di Michelino that portrays so magnificently the poet's pilgrimage through hell, purgatory, and heaven. I know I had seen it on our previous visit, but this time, as a result of my own journey into midlife and some of those darker regions of the soul, I stared at it with new appreciation and love.

Tuesday, November 15

Yesterday we made a pilgrimage to the city of Siena which, like Assisi, is built on hills. Ever since I began teaching about the writings of St. Catherine, I have wanted to visit the tomb of the woman whom Paul VI had declared a doctor of the church, and who had so bravely challenged the papacy on the need for reform. Today we toured Florence—at a much more leisurely pace than when we were here on our honeymoon. At the Uffizi Gallery I discovered works of art that over the years have become favorites of mine. There were three pictures, however, I do not remember having seen before that I fell in love with immediately. The first was Starnina's "Thebaid," a large panel that shows medieval Pisa, with brown-robed friars in the countryside, Dominicans working the gardens, and anchorites and anchoresses in the mountains peaking out of caves and giving advice to those who visited them in their one-room cells. Although a medieval setting, it reminded me of the early desert and Celtic spiritual traditions that I had been studying with Benedicta, and how much they had influenced medieval and renaissance Italy. The second painting that attracted me was Botticelli's "St. Augustine in His Study" that shows the early church father writing in some sort of book or journal, with tattered sheets of paper (from a composition?) at his feet.

The third work, one that captured my attention the most, was Fra Angelico's painting entitled "Coronation of the Virgin." In it Mary and Jesus are seated on a circle of clouds, surrounded by the angels and saints as only Fra Angelico's shimmering colors of gold, red, blue, and green can portray. One can clearly see a mutuality between the two main figures, with the masculine and feminine portrayed as equals and friends. Beautiful! The trumpets of the angels are an intrinsic part of the picture, making this scene one of celebration and great joy. It is the church, the communion of angels and saints as it is meant to be. To me, it speaks of the need for an integration of those two sides of ourselves, not only in each of us, as I am personally discovering at midlife, but in the beloved community we call "church." And, of course, the angels brought to mind Patrick's soul friend Victor, and all those helping spirits who guide our lives.

Thursday, November 17

I am writing this on the train to Ravenna, the city Benedicta said I should visit if I had the chance to see the beautiful Byzantine mosaics. I have also wanted to go there, since it is the place where Dante found shelter during his exile from Florence, and where he completed the *Divine Comedy*. JoAnne and I got up at the crack of dawn to get this train, and it seems to be stopping at every station along the way. As I look out the windows at the beautiful fall scenes in the mountains, I am becoming more conscious of how different this land and culture are from those of Celtic origins. People here are definitely more verbally expressive and more vocal than in Ireland and England. The culture itself seems more sensual, for here in Italy there is the celebration of the body, the physical, the beautiful. Somehow we Christians need to bring the two together into a new reality that appreciates both body and soul as works of God and as creative sources of spirituality, not denigrating one (body) or ignoring the other (soul).

Italy is definitely the land of Dante, and there are reminders of him everywhere in Florence. Dante's *Divine Comedy* begins with his middle years which turned out to be his most creative, as well as his most painful. My own beginning of midlife was not in a dark wood so much as in a dream, and, now as middle years take over, I pray too that JoAnne and I will be happy in spite of the emotional and psychic pulls we both feel between family ties and each of our needs for autonomy and solitude.

Friday, November 18

This is a second honeymoon! We arrived in Venice in the early afternoon by train and took a water taxi to our hotel, located not far from where Vivaldi lived for some years. The sky is overcast once again, but, even with the cold weather that seems to penetrate to the bone, the autumn beauty of this city is striking. We immediately, after unpacking, went out to the shops and the Basilica San Marco with its onion-shaped roofs and treasures from Byzantium. I was reminded, as I stared at the Gold Altar Piece inlaid with numerous jewels, of Savas's remark that so much of this wealth had been stolen from the Eastern Orthodox Christians of Constantinople during the Crusades who still want it returned. In late afternoon as the sun receded, the Piazza San Marco, with the gondolas rocked by the incoming waves, was bathed in colors of pink, maroon, and gold. Another sight of extraordinary beauty! Despite the persistent pleas of gondoliers, obviously desperate for business, we did not go for a ride on the canals. Our budget couldn't afford the prices they were quoting. Maybe some day!

Monday, November 21

I am writing this on the train from Florence to Rome. We returned to Florence after Venice, and stayed at Mario's one last time. This ride seems to be taking forever (another milk train, I think) and we need to get to Rome, take a bus to the airport, fly out to London's Heathrow Airport, take a bus to Gatwick, and then finally fly out of there in the morning. The trip back makes me anticipate homecoming all the more. I can't wait to see my sons and my parents. I just want to be there!

I couldn't believe the sight leaving Florence this morning. It had been raining, and as the train picked up speed from the station, there appeared in the sky right outside of the city that I have come to love not one, but three rainbows, crossing the countryside in all their glorious display of colors. I couldn't believe my eyes. Is God trying to say something with them? One would have to be a total skeptic to miss an obvious point. I mean, one rainbow, you could chalk up to chance; two might make a person more attentive; but three rainbows! The number three, for the ancient Celts, pagan and Christian alike, was a sacred, mystical number. Surely the rainbows are signs of God's love for JoAnne and me over the last ten years of our life together, as well as of hope for the coming years. This second honeymoon has rekindled our love for each other, and, I hope, helped begin to heal some of the hurt and stress of the past.

Holy One, I am grateful for all of your many gifts and graces, experienced so profoundly this autumn and these past days in Italy. Please continue to be with us, and bring us safely home.

Early this morning, before rising to our last day here, I had the strangest dream:

I am in a church waiting for the eucharist to begin when a young woman, a friend of mine, is being led out of the sacristy by older priests. She has a defiant smile on her face, obviously hurt by the action, but nonetheless determined to return. I am angry. I feel a kinship with her and also am determined, especially because she is a friend, to make room for her in the sanctuary of the church. In the dream, as I attempt to bring her back, I meet resistance but realize that this is the right thing to do. I realize that when her form of ministry is denied, all of our ministries suffer.

The dream with its vivid colors and imagery, as well as disconcerting plot has left me wondering: what is its meaning, and why did it come when it did—on my last night in a city I associate with so much happiness, in the country where the body and soul, the masculine and feminine are so intertwined?

Tuesday, November 22

I am too tired to write, but want to say how good it is to be home again. My biggest fear flying back was that I wouldn't have a "second chance" to show my family and friends that I love them. I want to make a difference in their lives; I want them to know that I will try to be different as a result of what I've learned about myself during these wonderful/horrible days away.

My parents and Daniel met us at the airport, while John had stayed home to prepare a surprise welcome. I hugged each one of them, holding them close, finally being able to physically embrace them after the months of yearning to do so. And I noticed as I walked in the door that there, on the wall in the kitchen, John had put up a picture of me which he had drawn. It showed only my face with my glasses somewhat off-center, and beneath the portrait were the following words: "Missing: Ed Sellner; Last Seen: August 24, Seen Like This."

Friday, November 24

Yesterday was Thanksgiving, a day that had special meaning for me considering my safe return, and the sense I have that I have been given the chance to start over again. For so many reasons, I feel overwhelmed with gratitude: for the tremendous gift of my journeys that have revealed so much to me about a loving, trustworthy God; for the people in England, Wales, and Ireland who became my friends and mentors; for all those, especially JoAnne and the boys, who made my research and travels possible. I have been gone a long time from my loved ones, longer, really, than this past fall, and I want to show them how much I love them.

This morning as Mom and Dad and I sat for a moment alone in the kitchen with the boys watching cartoons on television in the other room and JoAnne upstairs, I turned to my parents and, without thinking, said to them: "I want you to know how sorry I am for any hurt I've caused you in my life." They just looked at me, unable to speak, but, from the expression on Dad's face and the tears in Mom's eyes, they knew and appreciated what I was trying to say. "I guess I always expected my parents to be perfect," I continued, "and when you weren't I was angry or resentful, too often blaming you for my own unhappiness....You haven't been perfect parents; no one is. But you've been good parents, loving parents all my life; I know that now. And I love you."

Monday, December 26

"I knew that you would come back early, Dad," John said to

me last night as we sat near the Christmas tree, the one that we had cut down together as a family in early December.

"How did you know?" I asked, surprised at his observation.

Without glancing up from the coloring he was doing, he replied, "I knew you would miss us too much."

The flames from our blazing hearth reflected on the frost-covered window panes, and through them one could faintly perceive the dark shadows of barren trees and mounds of glistening snow outside. Wisdom comes to us in all sorts of unexpected places, I thought, even, as Jesus told us long ago, out of the mouths of children.

Since my return, we have celebrated the holidays around our fireplace with family and friends, and I have had time to do my own reflecting while staring into its firey coals. Gretchen Berg was right: the hearth is where treasure can be found. Creative energies and wisdom are ours when we discover and begin to live out of the spiritual center of our lives.

EPILOGUE

We shall not cease from exploration
And the end of all our exploring
Will be to arrive where we started
And know the place for the first time.

T.S. Eliot, "Little Gidding," *Four Quartets*

It's been over a year ago since I left Oxford, the place where I experienced deep and aching loneliness, as well as great joy. In some ways the past year has been a hard one when friends and family members faced various forms of crisis, reminding all of us once again of our powerlessness, of the sacredness of human life, and of our true priorities. At the same time, it's been a good year too, as my process of soul-making continues. I'm spending more time with my sons, trying to be more present to them, looking more often, as Daniel says, into their eyes. John and I are much closer than we've ever been before, and Daniel doesn't hate me anymore (as he told me the day after our flight back from England and Italy). JoAnne and I, of course, still have our conflicts as couples do who have different careers, schedules, personalities. But we're learning, I think, to be more patient with each other, more forgiving of each other's very human foibles, more assertive in asking each other's help.

This past year I've also taken the initiative and made some trips with my sons back to where my parents live in their retirement. I've attempted to talk with Dad about his experience of my growing up and his perspective on our relationship. It's good to listen, for a change without judgment, and hear things, perhaps I'd heard before, but now hear and understand as if for the first time. It's good to spend more time with both Dad and Mom, getting to know them freed from my projections. I am also attempting to mend some fences—really, build some bridges—between my brother and sister and myself, realizing that since I left home so many years ago, I have never really gotten to know them very well. Reconciliation, I am learning, is an ongoing life-long process, one that definitely becomes more important as we grow older, get to know ourselves better, and more consciously attempt to see others and ourselves with the compassion and love that God does. As many of us find by the time we've entered midlife, it is essential to our spirituality that we be someone who eases others' pain, rather than being a source of it.

My life on the surface, some might say, has returned to "normal," yet there are important differences. Within me there is greater serenity than I've ever had before. The two sides of me, represented by Robert Kennedy and C.S. Lewis, still remain very much alive, but I am less driven by them and more appreciative of my own limited gifts and gifted limitations. I have come to accept that the active and contemplative sides which they represent will probably always remain an important part of me, and that the inner tensions between them can act as a source of creativity. I am also experiencing a deeper sense of joy than ever before, a joy that permeates my being even on my worst days of "Celtic gloom."

In retrospect, I see now that it was my dream figure, Cuthbert, who first signaled the absence of joy in my life, and, more importantly, provided a way to find it. I was drawn, not fully comprehending, to Oxford to do research, only to discover, that, really, I'd gone in search of soul: a better understanding and acceptance icon of Rublev's Holy Trinity that reminds me of my spiritual kinship with St. Theosevia's, Fairacres, and the Skreen. To pray to the saints, whom the ancient Christian Celts called "our oldest ancestors," to remember with gratitude all of those mentors and friends who have changed our lives so profoundly is to establish communion with them and with the Holy One who made us all. To remember those who have touched us is one of the most powerful forms of prayer. We do not necessarily have to go to the tombs of the saints in foreign lands, although I would be the first to admit there is great value in doing so. We can encounter them in prayer and receive continuing guidance from them. To consciously put ourselves in touch with them is to be more intimately connected with our past, our roots, our spiritual heritage, our souls, as well as the holiness of the present moment and the graciousness of God.

In the gratitude that emerges from our prayers, we are often led, it seems, joyfully to deeds of ministry that not only invite others to change, but often change us profoundly in the process. We also find the desire to share with one another the journeys of our lives and the stories of our survival. In that storytelling, we begin to perceive more clearly and experience more fully the mysterious reality of church, the communion of saints in all its rich diversity. As my dream on St. Cuthbert's Day revealed and as my pilgrimage experiences confirmed, somehow when we tell our stories with honesty and listen to each other with compassion, hope is born, and, despite the confusion, loneliness, or even despair, we are given intimations of God's love.